Amish Canning

And Preserving

Bible For The

Home Canner

*A Step By Step Process For Beginners With 150
Recipes On How To Can And Preserve Meat, Soup,
Sauces, Pickles, Fruits, Vegetables And Much More*

Emily Fisher

Published By:

Blue House Media

Emily Fisher's Books

Click below to Get In Touch with me

Follow Me On Facebook

Follow Me On Instagram

Dedication

To my family—Who would have thought that all those hours I spent in the kitchen attempting to assuage your prodigious hunger pangs would lead to this?

I am so glad to be your mom!

Also to my readers I'm grateful to you guys for taking the opportunity to purchase and read through this book.

I hope to see you in my next book, thanks!

Table Of Content

Other Books By Emily Fisher

Click the links below to view my best selling books on amazon;

- *Magnolia Bakery Cookbook For The Home Baker*
- *Tortilla Press Cookbook Made Easy*
- *The Unofficial Downton Abbey Afternoon Tea Cookbook*
- *Epoxy Resin Art Made Easy*
- *CBT Workbook For Healing PTSD*

Magnolia Bakery Cookbook For The Home Baker: 100+ Sweet And Savory

Amish Canning Cookbook For The Home Canner: A Step By Step Proven Process

Epoxy Resin Art Made Easy: Discover The Step By Step Proven Techniques With

The Unofficial Downton Abbey Afternoon Tea Cookbook: The Step By

Emily Fisher > All Books

+ Follow ⓘ   HOME   ABOUT   ALL BOOKS

CBT Workbook For Healing PTSD: Discover The Step By Step Proven...
☆☆☆☆☆ 1

Kindle Edition

$3⁹⁹ kindleunlimited

Other formats: Hardcover, Paperback

Tortilla Press Cookbook Made Easy: A Step By Step Guide On How To Use The...
☆☆☆☆☆ 1

Kindle Edition

$3⁹⁹ kindleunlimited

Tortilla Press Cookbook Made Easy: A Step By Step Guide On How To Use The...
☆☆☆☆☆ 5

Hardcover

$19⁹⁵

Other formats: Paperback

Chapter 1: History Of Canning

When we think of home canning, our mind's eye is quick to envision neat rows of jars lining pantry shelves, safely filled with food just waiting to be opened so we can prepare a variety of tasty meals for our dear families. From the excess of summer gardens come the ingredients for many appetizing feasts during the cold winter months. Let those winter storms blow in—we have the satisfaction of knowing that our families will be well nourished because our pantry shelves are filled with a bit of summer's abundance.

Canning our own food seems the epitome of the industrious homemaker, but canning did not begin as an answer to the housewife's problem of what to have for dinner. Instead, canning was developed as an answer to a question posed by war. In the late 1700s, Emperor Napoleon Bonaparte of France was concerned that his soldiers were not being fed well when they traveled long distances from home, and he realized that they needed a reliable method for keeping food safe to eat for long periods. So he offered a cash prize to the person who could develop a dependable method of food preservation.

Enter Nicolas Appert, a French candy maker, brewer, distiller, and chef. Appert discovered that when heat was applied to food in sealed glass bottles, the food was preserved. In the early 1800s, the French navy successfully experimented with foods preserved by heat on their long voyages. They ate preserved meat, vegetables, fruit, and milk. But it would take more than 50 years to provide the reason for why the canning process worked. Finally, Louis Pasteur demonstrated that the growth of microorganisms causes food spoilage, and that sealing food into jars or cans using high heat kills these microorganisms, thus rendering the canned food safe to eat months, and even years, later.

Several years after Appert's discovery, an Englishman by the name of Peter Durand figured out how to successfully seal food in tin-coated iron cans, and in 1813 the first commercial canning factory was established in England. These cans of food were very expensive, and a person needed a chisel and hammer to open the container, but even so, the food canning industry was launched. Canned food was largely used by the military and explorers, and it wasn't until the 1920s that home canning caught on with homemakers.

In 1858, a Philadelphia tinsmith named John Mason patented a glass "fruit jar," which incorporated threads at the jar's top along with matching threads on a metal band that was screwed down on top of a zinc lid with a rubber gasket. For the first time, a canning jar system was easy to use and within reach of even modest budgets. Then in 1882, the Lightning jar was introduced. These glass jars had glass lids that used metal clamps to hold the lid and a rubber gasket in place. Atlas jars also used this system. In fact, the Lightning-type jar system was manufactured in the United States until the

1960s, and European companies still manufacture these jars (Weck and Leifheit are two such companies). They are very beautiful jars that come in many shapes and sizes.

Meanwhile, in the United States, Ball jars (1886) and Kerr jars (1903) began being made with the two-piece rings and lids we are used to seeing today. The metal lid came with a permanently attached gasket that sealed the food inside the jars. The companies were eventually combined, and today the Jarden Corporation manufactures and sells Ball, Kerr, Bernardin (sold mostly in Canada), and Golden Harvest jars.

One other development of note occurred in 1976 when Stieg Tattler reusable lids went on the market. During the 1960s and 1970s, at the height of the "back to the land" movement, there was such a resurgence of interest in home canning that jars and lids were often hard to come by, and the introduction of Tattler reusables was a direct result of this dearth. Tattler lids are made from a dense plastic compound that is BPA-free. A reusable rubber ring or gasket makes the seal.

Tattler lids and rubber rings have been shown to last twenty years or more, and often after many years of use, the only replacements needed are the rubber rings.

Even though the canning process itself has changed little over the last two hundred years, research and trials led by universities and government agencies have honed the safety guidelines for specific foods being canned, and these are constantly being updated as needed. So even though you may have a recipe that has been handed down from your beloved grandmother or aunt, it's best to rely on the most up-to-date data available. You can probably still use that old-time favorite recipe, but you may need to change the processing time or method. For the sake of your family's safety, you'll be well advised to do so.

Chapter 2: Getting Started

There are two basic canning methods—boiling water-bath canning and pressure canning. And essentially, there are two groups of foods—high-acid foods with a pH of 4.6 or lower and low-acid (alkaline) foods, with a pH of more than 4.6. High-acid foods generally use the water-bath method and low-acid foods require pressure canning at higher-than-boiling temperatures to render them safe.

Following is an overview of the process for each method, but in the following chapters I'll go into more detail, with specific, step-by-step instructions that you can follow when you are actually canning.

Boiling Water-Bath Canners

Boiling water-bath canning is used for high-acid foods such as jam, jelly, fruit butter, preserves, and marmalade; fruit pieces, fruit juice, and fruit pie filling; tomatoes, plain tomato sauce, and tomato juice (lemon juice or some other acidifier is added to tomato products to ensure that the acid level is high enough to safely can these foods with the boiling water-bath method); and pickles and relishes.

Any large pot with a tight-fitting lid will do, but water-bath canners made especially for canning foods are inexpensive and sized appropriately and are well worth the small investment. You will need a rack that sits on the bottom to keep the jars up from the floor of the pot, and the pot must be tall enough that the jars are covered by 2 inches of water with another 1 to 2 inches of air space above that. You can also use a pressure canner for water-bath canning as long as it is tall enough.

After you have prepared the food you plan on canning, fill the jars with the food or liquid, screw the lids and rings on, and then set them into the canner to which you have added enough hot water to fill it halfway. Once all your jars are in place, add more hot water if necessary to cover the jars by two inches. Cover and heat the canner until the water comes to a rolling boil (212°F, 100°C). Once a rolling boil has been achieved you will begin the processing time, which can be anywhere from 5 minutes to 1½ hours. During the processing time you can lower the heat a bit, but make sure that the water never stops boiling during the entire processing period.

Boiling the jars in the water removes the oxygen. This helps form a tight seal and is sufficient to kill the mold, yeast, and bacterial cells present in the food. And even though boiling at 212° doesn't kill the clostridium botulinum spores— which cause botulism, a potentially deadly toxin—the high acid levels in foods with a pH that is 4.6 or less doesn't allow the spores to grow. Therefore, the canned food is safe to consume.

Many people prefer to "get their feet wet" by water-bath canning before they take the plunge into pressure canning. But that's really just a matter of preference (or possibly courage!), because pressure canning is just as simple—in fact, pressure canning green beans is probably the easiest food of all to preserve.

Pressure Canners

Pressure canning at temperatures higher than 212°F (100°C) is required for vegetables, meat, poultry, fish and seafood, and combination recipes that include low-acid foods. This is because the pH level is too high in these low-acid foods to prevent the growth of clostridium botulinum, which is the microorganism that causes botulism. When the spores are in an anaerobic environment (lacking oxygen, as happens to jars of food that are canned) they are able to grow and produce deadly levels of botulism toxin. Therefore, pressure is needed to raise the temperature, and pressure canning does that, raising the temperature inside the container to 240°F. When correctly processed for adequate periods of time, the botulinum spores are eliminated and the canned food is safe to store and eventually eat.

Unlike a water-bath canner, you will need to invest in a specially made pressure canner. And while the purchase price of a pressure canner isn't small, this is an investment that will last you for many years when properly maintained. There are two types of pressure canners—those that use a gasket to close and seal the lids after they have been locked into place (such as the Presto brand), and those that are "gasketless" and seal by use of heavy-duty screws that tighten the locked lid to the body of the canner (such as the All American). The gasket canners generally cost less than the gasketless types, but you will need to replace the gaskets every year or so, depending on how much you use it. Gaskets cost less than 10 dollars, so this is a small additional expense, and with the money you saved on the purchase price compared to the gasketless types, you will still be ahead even after many years of use.

Pressure canners are also fitted with a dial or weighted gauge that indicates when the desired pressure (that is, psi, or pounds per square inch) has been reached inside the canner. Dial gauges must be watched during the entire time food is being processed to make sure the psi doesn't fall below the recommended level. Also, you must test your dial gauge every year to make sure it still gives an accurate reading. On the other hand, weighted gauges exhaust small amounts of steam during the entire processing period, causing the weighted gauge to rock back and forth, so you won't need to constantly be checking the gauge visually—instead, you'll be able to know that the pressure is at the correct psi simply by hearing the rocking of the gauge, and this will allow you to move about more instead of being stuck close to the stove for long periods as when using a dial gauge. Another plus of the weighted gauge system is that unless you damage the gauge, you won't need to get it tested annually.

One more point to make regarding the weighted gauges: They usually come with a one-piece gauge weighted at 15 psi, but you can buy a three-piece gauge that adjusts to 5, 10, or 15 psi. These three-piece gauges are the easiest to use and allow the most freedom of movement during processing because if you are processing at 10 psi, you will be able to hear the rocking and know without looking that all is well.

Equipment Needed

There are several other items that you will need in order to successfully can.

Canning Jars

There are numerous canning jars available in many different sizes and shapes, from 4 ounces to a half-gallon, but the most popular sizes are half-pints, pints, and quarts. In fact, the half-gallon sizes shouldn't be used for anything other than apple or grape juice, but they do make great storage jars for such things as sugar, beans, oatmeal, and the like. Jar openings are either regular or wide-mouth, no matter how much the jar holds. Only use jars made specifically for canning, as they have been properly tempered and breakage in the canner is kept to a minimum. Mayonnaise or empty food jars aren't safe to use as stand-ins for commercially made canning jars. (And yes, people will tell you they successfully use recycled mayonnaise jars, but it's not recommended.)

Lids

The most common lids come in two pieces—the metal lid has a ring of sealing compound around the edge, and a screw band holds the lid in place while processing. There are also reusable lids (Tattlers by Stieg) that work much the same way as the two-piece lids but are said to last twenty years. The reusables cost more initially, but if you can food regularly, they will more than pay for themselves over time. There are also jars that have odd sizes and use different lid systems, but they are not common in most stores and must be bought online. Still, some of them are beauties—though expensive—and might be just the thing for a special home-canned gift or your prized recipe.

The lids come in regular or wide-mouth sizes, and they correspond to the regular or wide-mouth canning jars. You can't interchange them; you will need to have on hand the correct size depending on the jar you use. You will use far more lids than screw bands (unless you choose to use the Tattler reusables) because lids should only be used one time, while the screw bands can be used again and again until they rust or get dented.

Air Bubble Remover

You can use a plastic (no metal!) knife of the sort that you would take on a picnic and they work great, but you can also buy a bubble remover/headspace measurer that works just as well. One end of this handy tool is tapered to slide around the insides of the jars to dislodge bubbles before putting the lid on, and the other end has graduated notches that show fill lines from ¼ to 1 inch.

Funnel

A plastic funnel fits into the jars and makes filling them neat and easy. Funnels are especially useful when packing hot food or liquid into the jars. Canning funnels are made to fit both wide-mouth and regular size jars; you'll only need one.

Jar Lifter

Jar lifters are useful for carrying full jars in and out of the canner without touching them and burning yourself. They look like wide tongs with rubber grips that securely hold jars while you move them about. I consider a jar lifter a necessity.

Magnetic Lid Lifter or Tongs

Magnetic lid lifters are a pencil-shaped tool with a magnet at one end that is used to remove lids from hot water. Specially manufactured tongs for canning are made and are longer than what's usually available in the kitchen tool department. You'll find them wherever canning supplies are sold.

Small Notebook

It's a good idea to keep notes of everything you preserve. Handy information includes the date, amount of food harvested (in pounds, quarts, etc.), variety (in the case of fruits and vegetables), recipe used, and number and size of jars yielded. This type of information can be invaluable in future years as you are deciding how much of something you want to can for the coming year. Plus, it's very satisfying to read through your canning "diary" and remember what you've preserved over the years. This is the place to make whatever notes and interesting tidbits you'd like to recollect.

Of course, there are many more tools you can take advantage of to make your canning jobs easier. Depending on what foods you choose to process, there are juicers, strainers, cherry pitters, slicers, and food mills. And while these tools can make your job easier and quicker, they aren't necessary to get the work done. But if you find that you enjoy canning, you'll probably collect these handy tools over time. I think they are worth every penny I've spent over the years as I've built up my collection of useful gadgets.

Chapter 3: Water-Bath Canning

Processing times will vary depending on the particular food you are canning, but the steps you take to end up with safely processed jars will always be the same. And no matter how much you can, having these instructions before you each time will ensure that you don't forget an important step and run the risk of improperly canned food or jars that fail to seal.

Inspect Your Canner

Making sure all parts are in good working condition. There should be no dents or warping of the canner base. If the rack that holds the filled jars has corroded from prior usage, buy a new one. (You'd hate to have it fail when you're lifting out a heavy load of hot jars.) Wash your canner and lid.

Inspect And Wash Your Jars, Lids, And Screw Bands

Make sure your jars aren't chipped or cracked, the lids have a complete ring of sealing compound around the edge, and the bands aren't bent or rusted. Wash jars in hot soapy water or put them through a complete regular cycle in your dishwasher, leaving the jars in the closed dishwasher until ready to use. If hand washing them, rinse the jars after washing and place them in a pot with water to cover. Simmer them in the water until ready to use. Alternatively, you can place your jars on a cookie sheet and place them in a 175-degree oven until needed.

Lids need to be washed with hot soapy water, rinsed, and placed in another pot with water to cover. Simmer the lids in the water, but don't let the water boil, as this could compromise the sealing compound and result in a sealing failure. You want to see tiny bubbles in the pot, but that's all.

Wash the bands in hot soapy water, rinse and dry them, and then set them aside until needed. Or you can put the bands in the pot of water with the lids already nesting in them, ready to lift out when closing up the jars of food.

Place Canner On Stove

Fill your water-bath canner halfway with water, place the canner on your largest burner, and turn on the heat so the water is very hot but not boiling. Place the canner rack into the canner or set the rack handles on the top edge of the canner if you have that type of rack (most water-bath canners come with a rack included).

Fill Jars

Fill one jar at a time. You will complete the filling process steps below and cap the jar before moving on to the next jar and repeating the process: a. Fill the jar with food and any liquid used. Pack the jars well, but don't smash the food.

- Measure headspace. Headspace is the space between the jar's top rim and the top of the food or liquid. In general, you will leave 1 inch of headspace for low-acid foods (meat, vegetables, poultry, beans, and fish); ½ inch of headspace for high-acid foods such as tomatoes and fruits; and ⅛–¼ inch of headspace for juices, jams, jellies, and pickles.

- Remove air bubbles. Run a plastic knife or air bubble tool around the sides of the jar to dislodge bubbles. Don't neglect this step even if you think there are no air bubbles present. If you forget this step, don't worry—your food will still be safe, but occasionally bubbles will cause jars to not seal. Generally, I'll insert the knife along the side of the jar and then gently press toward the middle. I do this about 3 or 4 times, inserting the knife at a new spot each time.

- Clean jar rims. A wet paper towel works great for cleaning jar rims. Run the wet paper towel or a wet washcloth around the top of the jar. You want to make sure there are no pieces of food or spices clinging to the top edge because the sealing compound must be in contact all the way around the jar top in order for the jar to seal properly.

- Screw on lids and bands. Place the lid on the jar, sealing side down so it's in contact with the jar rim, and then screw on the band. You want to screw it on quite snug, but don't overtighten it—there's no need to crank down as hard as you can. "Finger-tip tight" is how the tightness rule is often stated. Note regarding use of Tattlers: If you are using Tattlers, refer to chapter 5 for information on how to screw on the Tattler plastic lids—it's a bit different than when using the more common two-piece system.

- Place filled jar in canner rack. Using the jar lifter so you don't burn yourself, place your filled jar into the canner's rack. As you add jars, remember to keep them balanced by placing jars opposite each other instead of placing them side-by-side and running the risk of the rack toppling. I generally start by placing the first jar in the middle slot of the canner rack as that seems to help with balancing out the weight when I continue adding jars.

Prepare The Canner For Processing

When your entire load is in place, lower the rack with the filled jars into the canner. (You may need to use hot pads for this step.) Add simmering water if needed to cover the jars by 1–2 inches. Turn the heat to medium-high, place the lid on the canner, and bring the water to a full rolling boil.

Processing And Adjusting For Altitude

When the water in the canner has come to a full rolling boil, set the timer according to the recipe's processing time. However, you'll need to adjust the processing times depending on what the altitude is where you live. The increased processing times are as follows:

Altitude in Feet	Increased Processing Time
0 – 1,000	No adjustment in minutes
1,001 – 3,000	5 minutes
3,001 – 6,000	10 minutes
6,001 – 8,000	15 minutes
8,001 – 10,000	20 minutes

During this processing period it is necessary to ensure that the water never stops boiling. Also, the level of the boiling water should never drop below the top of the lids; you can add boiling water if necessary to maintain fully covered jars. When the processing time is complete, turn off the heat and remove the canner lid. (Don't forget to use hot mitts and lift the lid so the steam releases away from you.) Let the jars sit in the opened canner for about 5 minutes before removing them. Next, place the jars on a dry towel or wooden cutting board with air space between them and let them sit undisturbed until completely cool. Do not push down on the center of the lid and don't tighten the bands.

Note: If using Tattler reusable lids, you must tighten down the screw bands immediately upon taking the jars out of the canner. Make sure you use oven mitts because the contents are boiling hot.

Give the screw bands a good hard crank.

Check Jars For Proper Seal

You know the jars are sealed when the small dome area in the middle of the lid pops down. This can happen with a loud popping noise (very gratifying!), or it can be a slower process, but once the dome is pulled down the jar is sealed. If, after several hours, you notice the dome in the middle of a lid is still up (meaning the jar hasn't sealed), it's a good idea to put that jar in the refrigerator and use the food within several days. Or you can reprocess the food using a new lid and the same processing time as before.

After about 12 hours, check each jar to make sure it has a good seal: Remove the bands and then press on the lid to make sure the center is tight and concave (curved slightly downward).

Carefully lift the jar by the edge of the lid with your fingers. The lid should hold. Next, wipe the jars with a damp cloth to clean them. Write on the lid or attach a label to the jar that indicates what's inside. It's also a good idea to add the date so you can eat your older jars of food first.

Note: Because Tattler lids are made using a hard plastic, the lids won't pop down so there's no visual indication that a seal has been made. After about 12 hours, or once the jar of food has thoroughly cooled, you will need to remove the screw band and then gently lift the jar by the rim to check for a proper seal. If the seal has been made, you will be able to lift the jar by the plastic seal without it coming off.

Wash Your Canner And Tools

Make sure everything is bone dry before closing up the canner and storing it.

Chapter 4: Pressure Canning

Processing times will vary depending on the particular food you are canning, but the steps you take to end up with safely processed jars will always be the same.

Inspect Your Canner

Making sure all parts are in good working condition. There should be no dents or warping of the canner base. If the rack that holds the filled jars has corroded from prior usage, buy a new one. (You'd hate to have it fail when you're lifting out a heavy load of hot jars.) Wash your canner and lid.

Inspect And Wash Your Jars, Lids, And Screw Bands

Make sure your jars aren't chipped or cracked, the lids have a complete ring of sealing compound around the edge, and the bands aren't bent or rusted. Wash jars in hot soapy water or put them through a complete regular cycle in your dishwasher, leaving the jars in the closed dishwasher until ready to use. If hand washing them, rinse the jars after washing and place them in a pot with water to cover. Simmer them in the water until ready to use. Alternatively, you can place your jars on a cookie sheet and place them in a 175-degree oven until needed.

Lids need to be washed with hot soapy water, rinsed, and placed in another pot with water to cover. Simmer the lids in the water, but don't let the water boil, as this could compromise the sealing compound and result in a sealing failure. You want to see tiny bubbles in the pot, but that's all.

Wash the bands in hot soapy water, rinse and dry them, and then set them aside until needed. Or you can put the bands in the pot of water with the lids already nesting in them, ready to lift out when closing up the jars of food.

Place Canner On Stove

Fill your water-bath canner halfway with water, place the canner on your largest burner, and turn on the heat so the water is very hot but not boiling. Place the canner rack into the canner or set the rack handles on the top edge of the canner if you have that type of rack (most water-bath canners come with a rack included).

Fill Jars

Fill one jar at a time. You will complete the filling process steps below and cap the jar before moving on to the next jar and repeating the process: a. Fill the jar with food and any liquid used. Pack the jars well, but don't smash the food.

- Measure headspace. Headspace is the space between the jar's top rim and the top of the food or liquid. In general, you will leave 1 inch of headspace for low-acid foods (meat, vegetables, poultry, beans, and fish); ½ inch of headspace for high-acid foods such as tomatoes and fruits; and ⅛–¼ inch of headspace for juices, jams, jellies, and pickles.

- Remove air bubbles. Run a plastic knife or air bubble tool around the sides of the jar to dislodge bubbles. Don't neglect this step even if you think there are no air bubbles present. If you forget this step, don't worry—your food will still be safe, but occasionally bubbles will cause jars to not seal. Generally, I'll insert the knife along the side of the jar and then gently press toward the middle. I do this about 3 or 4 times, inserting the knife at a new spot each time.

- Clean jar rims. A wet paper towel works great for cleaning jar rims. Run the wet paper towel or a wet washcloth around the top of the jar. You want to make sure there are no pieces of food or spices clinging to the top edge because the sealing compound must be in contact all the way around the jar top in order for the jar to seal properly.

- Screw on lids and bands. Place the lid on the jar, sealing side down so it's in contact with the jar rim, and then screw on the band. You want to screw it on quite snug, but don't overtighten it—there's no need to crank down as hard as you can. "Finger-tip tight" is how the tightness rule is often stated. Note regarding use of Tattlers: If you are using Tattlers, refer to chapter 5 for information on how to screw on the Tattler plastic lids—it's a bit different than when using the more common two-piece system.

- Place filled jar in canner rack. Using the jar lifter so you don't burn yourself, place your filled jar into the canner's rack. As you add jars, remember to keep them balanced by placing jars opposite each other instead of placing them side-by-side and running the risk of the rack toppling. I generally start by placing the first jar in the middle slot of the canner rack as that seems to help with balancing out the weight when I continue adding jars.

Prepare The Canner For Processing

When your entire load is in place, put the lid on the canner, making sure that the handles line up so the lid can lock. (The instruction manual that came with your canner will guide you to properly closing the lid on your particular model.) Turn the heat to medium- high. Do not yet put the pressure regulator on the vent pipe!

Exhaust The Air From The Canner

Heat the canner and contents until a steady flow of steam escapes from the vent pipe in the lid. You can't always see the steam escaping, but you can hear it and feel it. But be careful! Putting your hand too close to the escaping steam will burn your hand. Let the steam escape through the vent pipe for 7 to 10 minutes. It's okay to reduce the heat, but make sure the steam continues to vent during those 10 minutes.

Place The Pressure Regulator On The Vent Pipe

Once the pressure regulator has been placed on the vent pipe, you can turn the heat up fairly high. As pressure builds inside the canner, you will see the pointer in the gauge start to move. When the pressure registers the correct psi, you can lower the heat to maintain the correct pressure as follows:

Altitude in Feet	Weighted Gauge	Dial Gauge
0 – 1,000	10	11
1,001 – 2,000	15	11
2,001 – 4,000	15	12
4,001 – 6,000	15	13
6,001 – 8,000	15	14
8,001 – 10,000	15	15

Processing

When the correct pressure has been reached, set your timer according to the recipe directions. Check your gauge often to verify that the pressure never goes down below the correct psi. If it does, you'll need to begin the timing all over again. Once the psi reaches the correct level you can turn down the heat a bit to maintain the psi. Make small adjustments to see what happens to the pressure instead of turning the burner way down all at once.

Cooling Period

When the processing time is complete, turn off the heat and move the pressure canner to another burner to cool. Do not remove the weighted gauge from the vent pipe or unfasten the lid! Allow the pressure inside the canner to come down to zero on its own. When the pressure reads zero, wait another 5 minutes before you remove the weighted gauge and then carefully remove the lid, making sure to lift in such a way that the steam escapes away from your face. Use oven mitts and work carefully.

Remove Jars From Canner

Using oven mitts and your jar lifter, place the jars on a towel or wooden cutting board, spaced about an inch apart so the air can circulate around them. Do not tighten the bands. Let the jars continue to cool naturally until they are completely cool.

Note: If using Tattler reusable lids, you must tighten down the screw bands immediately upon taking the jars out of the canner. Make sure you use oven mitts because the contents are boiling hot. Give the screw bands a good hard crank

Check Jars For Proper Seal

You know the jars are sealed when the small dome area in the middle of the lid pops down. This can happen with a loud popping noise (very gratifying!), or it can be a slower process, but once the dome is pulled down, the jar is sealed. If, after several hours, you notice the dome in the middle of a lid is still up (meaning the jar hasn't sealed), it's a good idea to put that jar in the refrigerator and use the food within several days. Or you can reprocess the food using a new lid.

After about 12 hours, check each jar to make sure it has a good seal: Remove the bands and then press on the lid to make sure the center is tight and concave (curved slightly downward). Carefully lift the jar by the edge of the lid with your fingers. The lid should hold. Next, wipe the jars with a damp cloth to clean them. Write on the lid or attach a label to the jar that indicates what's inside. It's also a good idea to add the date so you can eat your older jars of food first.

Note: Because Tattler lids are made using a hard plastic, the lids won't pop down so there's no visual indication that a seal has been made. After about 12 hours, or once the jar of food has thoroughly cooled, you will need to remove the screw band and then gently lift the jar by the rim to check for a proper seal. If the seal has been made, you will be able to lift the jar by the plastic seal without it coming off.

Alright, guys please before we move to the next chapter, if you're truly getting value from this book, please don't hesitate to leave your honest review. Thanks! Also if you're a fan of the Magnolia Bakery I've put together a book that contains all of the best recipes from the magnolia bakery. I will drop the link at the end of this book. Thanks again.

Chapter 5: Tattler Reusable Canning Lids

Tattler reusable canning lids and rubber rings can be used for about twenty years before you need to replace the rubber rings—and the food-safe plastic lids can last even longer. They can be used with water-bath or pressure canning and are especially useful when canning high-acid foods such as pickles because the hard plastic lids won't corrode over time.

The white plastic lids are thicker than the usual two-piece lids, and the gaskets are quite thin and narrow. You use a regular screw band of the type that comes with Ball and Kerr jars to place the lids on your canning jars. (These can be purchased separately wherever canning supplies are available.)

When using Tattlers, you don't have a visual indication that a seal has been made until you actually remove the screw band and lift the jar to see if the seal was made. This means that the food sits in the jars until completely cool whether or not a seal has been made. This shouldn't be a problem, but if you discover that a jar hasn't sealed, immediately refrigerate the contents, reprocess, or eat it.

My Experience With Tattlers

When I started reading about Tattler reusable lids, I was curious—the notion that I might never need to buy lids again was appealing because I can hundreds of jars of food every year, and it didn't take much math to figure that I could save money in the long run by using them. So I set about to buy some boxes of lids and gaskets and began to experiment.

As it happened, my canning project on the day I first used Tattlers was ground beef. I can a lot of meat because I appreciate having ready-made meal ingredients for those evenings when I'm in a hurry to put food on the table or when I'm tired and want my version of "fast food." But meat is also something that I no longer produce for myself—I must spend some of my hard-earned money to buy the meats that I consume, quite unlike the fruits and vegetables I can grow virtually free.

I know my canning stuff. So I figured that I wouldn't have any problem tackling Tattlers.

How wrong I was.

I filled 9 pint jars with ground beef and then placed the Tattlers on the jars according to the package directions, which read, *"Screw band on jar loosely. Center lid on jar and hold in place with finger while tightening the metal screw band finger-tip tight. Do not overtighten. Product must be allowed to vent during processing."*

Those directions seemed straightforward when I read them, but I quickly realized that "finger-tip tight" was subjective. What, I wondered, did "finger-tip tight" actually entail? Not easily daunted, I screwed the lids on, placed the jars in my pressure canner, and processed them. I was feeling pretty smug, thinking about all the money I planned on saving over the next twenty years.

Processing complete. Screw bands immediately tightened, per instructions. Cooling period over. Now came the exciting part—to remove the screw bands and test for a seal. It never occurred to me that I could run into any difficulty... but I did. I had slightly more than a 40 percent failure rate. That amounts to four of my nine jars not sealing. I was flabbergasted and more than a little frustrated.

So I researched some more. I called the helpful folks at Tattler and I got online and read blog posts about other people's experiences. After a lot of input, I decided to try using Tattlers again. But for the next several loads, I only did half the load with Tattlers and half the usual way with the two-piece rings and seals. I had success, and I'm growing to like reusables very much.

Basic Tips for Success

Basically you'll either be using Tattlers correctly, or not. And there is a learning curve, so don't get frustrated if you experience sealing failures in the beginning like I did. Keep tweaking your procedure and you'll eventually figure out what works for your personal canning style. The crux of canning with Tattlers seems to come when tightening the lids on the jars before processing, so that is the step you should think about and change up slightly if you have problems. To help you get a feel for this step, here are different ways to say the same thing—that is, how to successfully tighten the band in order to produce a seal when using a Tattler:

- Put the lid on the jar and hold it in place with your finger while tightening the metal screw band finger-tip tight. Don't overtighten as the food in the jar needs to vent during processing.

- Place the lid and screw band on the jar and screw it in place just like you do your regular two-piece lids. Then back off and loosen the screw band about a quarter of an inch so the food can vent during processing.

- Place the lid and screw band on the jar and tighten the band just until the grooves catch on the ridges of the jar. Don't screw on tight because the food needs to vent during processing.

Hopefully one of these descriptions will resonate and you won't have a rocky beginning like I had.

You might want to consider canning half your load with Tattlers and half your load with regular two-piece lids and bands until you're comfortable using them. That way, if you experience seal failure while you're learning you won't have multiple jars of unsealed food to eat in a hurry.

You can also practice using Tattlers by filling them with water and simply canning a few trial loads to see what your success rate is. That way you won't be wasting food if the jars don't seal. Keep at it until you have successfully canned several complete canner loads with all the jars sealed.

How To Remove Lids

When opening jars of food that have been canned with the regular two-piece rings and seals, it's a simple matter to grab a bottle opener and pop the lid off the jar. But with Tattlers, you'll need to do things a bit differently once again.

Because you want to save and reuse the plastic lids and gaskets, you must exercise care when opening your jars. Here's how Tattler describes the process:

"When removing lid, gently insert table knife between rubber and jar to release seal—do not use sharp knife."

I tried this and it wasn't too easy because I couldn't get a sturdy purchase between the lid and the seal—there's just no room. And when I finally managed to open the lid, the liquid inside the jar splashed out. I tried opening the jar with a bottle opener and that worked, but I was concerned about using a semi-sharp metal tool due to Tattler's warning of "do not use sharp knife." So I went to the store and found a plastic bottle opener which was advertised as being useful for people who have arthritis in their hands. It's made of thick plastic instead of metal and is wider and thicker than its metal counterpart. It also has a plastic pry area, and I thought that would open my jars without the threat of breaking or warping the plastic lids or tearing the gasket. So far, so good—it seems to work well, and I will continue to use it.

So are Tattler reusable lids something you should consider? I think they definitely have their place in the canning kitchen. The fact that you can buy a quantity and then use them again and again is definitely a plus. Your budget will take a hit only once and then you'll always have your supplies at hand—no running to the store at the last minute to buy more lids when you run low. Being prepared is always good. I have Tattlers and I use them.

But I also keep a large supply of the Ball and Kerr two-piece lids and bands on hand, and I use those regularly. I love them for their ease of use and their ready availability in most stores.

Experiment and decide for yourself if Tattlers have a place in your own kitchen. You may be pleased with the results.

Chapter 6: Butters, Jams, And Jellies

Amish women can numerous jars of butters, jams, jellies, and preserves during the harvest months. Fruit is most often grown on their property, and preserving the abundance in season makes good sense. When the winter snow flies those jars of jellied goodness will enhance many a meal, and families will delight in the lingering taste of summer.

In days gone by, before commercially packaged pectin was available, jellied food was made by extracting the juice or crushing the fruit and then adding sugar and cooking the syrup down until it was done. But results could vary widely: the riper the fruit used, the less pectin was present; and overcooking (easy to do) meant that the jam or jelly tasted burnt. And sometimes a farmwife might overcook her fruit and end up with syrup instead of jam or jelly without meaning to. You can still make jams and jellies this way, but using packaged pectin is easier—the process doesn't take as long and your results, while still occasionally surprising, are much better.

Butters

Fruit butters are an old-fashioned delight. They use less sugar than jams and jellies and the fruit is cooked without adding in pectin. Rather, the naturally occurring pectin that is found in fruits is what allows the butters to thicken and jell. As a result, fruit butters are generally more spreadable than jams or jellies. Another plus is that fruit butters can be made using less than perfect fruit such as windfall apples and pears that haven't started to rot. You will, however, want to cut out any bruised spots or rotten areas.

The process for making fruit butter is to first cook the fruit to make pulp. Then you will add sugar and spices to the pulp and continue to cook until it's ready to can. Fruit butter is easy to prepare, but it does take time to complete the cooking process.

Apples

Quarter apples. No need to core or peel them. (Much of an apple's natural pectin is found in the core.) Add half as much apple juice or cider as you have fruit.

Apricots

Remove pits and then crush the fruit. Add half as much water or juice as you have fruit.

Grapes

Remove stems and then crush the fruit. No need to add additional liquid.

Peaches

Peel by immersing peaches in boiling water for approximately 30– 60 seconds or until the skin loosens easily. Remove pits and then crush the fruit. No need to add additional liquid.

Pears

Remove stem and blossom ends. Peel if desired. Quarter and core the pears and then crush the fruit. No need to add additional liquid.

Plums

Remove pits and then crush the fruit. No need to add additional liquid.

Preparing

- Cook your prepared fruit, stirring frequently so it doesn't scorch or stick to the pan. The fruit needs to be cooked until it is very soft and seems thick. This can take an hour or more. Next, run the cooked fruit through a sieve or food mill to puree the pulp and remove the peelings, seeds, etc.

- Add ½ to 1 tsp. ground cinnamon per quart of pulp and ⅛ tsp. per quart of any other spices you wish to use, such as allspice, cloves, nutmeg, and ginger.

- Place the puree in a large, heavy kettle (a thin-walled pot will tend to scorch the butter as it cooks). The kettle must have high enough sides that the butter won't boil over when cooking down, and the broader the base of the kettle, the more evaporation will be able to take place, thus producing a thick butter in less time.

- Cook the butter over medium low heat, stirring constantly, until sugar is dissolved and the fruit begins to boil. Continue cooking, stirring very frequently, until the butter thickens. The butter is ready when it rounds slightly on a spoon and has a glossy sheen.

- When the butter is ready, you are now ready to can it. Pack the hot butter into sterilized hot pint jars, leaving ¼ inch headspace. Place the lids and bands on and process in a boiling water-bath canner for 10 minutes.

Apple butter is probably the most often-made fruit butter, and cinnamon is the usual spice that is added. When making pear butter, try adding nutmeg or ginger for a tasty variation. And when you make grape, peach, or apricot, there's no need to add any additional spices—they are good as is. Cook's choice!

Fruit/Applesauce Butter

- 8 cups applesauce
- 1 large package Jell-O (i.e., strawberry or raspberry)
- 1 small package unflavored gelatin (optional)

Preparing

Dissolve Jell-O in ½ cup boiling water and dissolve unflavored gelatin in ½ cup cold water, if using. Mix together and then add the applesauce; heat to a simmer and then put the fruit/applesauce butter into pint jars and process them in a boiling water-bath for 10 minutes

Jams

Fruit jams make a wonderful addition to your menus, and in Amish kitchens you'll often find bread and jam or jelly at most meals because they help to "fill in the corners" of big appetites. Jams also make great toppings for pancakes, biscuits, angel food cake, and even ice cream.

Whereas jelly is made from fruit juice, jam is made using crushed fruit. Jam is generally softer than jelly, and while it will more or less hold its shape when spooned onto a piece of bread, it can be easily spread, even on a delicate item. Plus, you won't need as much fruit to make a batch of jam because you will be using the fruit meat instead of just the juice. Also, you can use frozen fruit that has been thawed, so your options are even greater.

How To Make Jam Without Adding Pectin

There are a number of ways to test for doneness when cooking jam, but to my way of thinking, the most reliable method is this:

- Using a candy thermometer, first boil a pot of plain water. Insert the thermometer into the boiling water to determine the actual temperature. Water boils at slightly different temperatures depending on your elevation and the current atmospheric conditions. So, to be as accurate as possible, it's a good idea to take the temperature of boiling water each time you are planning to make jam.

- In a very large pot, mix together the crushed fruit and sugar according to the recipes below and then bring the mixture to a boil, stirring very frequently. Keep the heat fairly low until the sugar has completely dissolved and then turn the heat up to cook the jam rapidly. When the temperature of the jam has risen 9 degrees higher than the temperature at which the plain water boiled, it has reached its jelling point and is now ready to be processed. Immediately take the pot off the heat.

- Let the jam sit for 4 to 5 minutes, gently stirring frequently so you won't create air bubbles in the jam. This will help the bits of fruit to suspend throughout the jam instead of collecting at the top.

- Ladle jam into hot sterilized pint or half-pint jars, leaving ¼-inch headspace. Screw on the lids and bands and process for 15 minutes in a boiling water-bath canner.

Jam Recipes With No Pectin

The following recipes are for making jam without adding packaged pectin. When you are selecting your fruit, try to have about a quarter of the amount needed a bit under-ripe. Slightly under-ripe fruit has more natural pectin than fully ripened fruit, and your jams will be thicker as a result.

If you don't mind some surprises along the way, you can try your hand at any fruit (or combinations of fruit) you have available. Keep notes on what worked and what didn't and develop your own recipes.

Apricot Jam

- 2 quarts peeled, pitted, and crushed apricots
- ¼ cup lemon juice
- 6 cups of sugar

Preparing

In a large pot, combine crushed apricots and lemon juice and stir to mix.

Add sugar and stir to mix and dissolve. Follow the directions for "How To Make Jam Without Added Pectin."

Berry Jam (Blackberry, blueberry, boysenberry, raspberry, etc.)

- 9 cups crushed berries
- 6 cups of sugar

Preparing

Follow the directions for "How To Make Jam Without Added Pectin."

Concord Grape Jam

- 2 quarts stemmed Concord grapes
- 6 cups sugar

Preparing

Pop the grapes from the skins and set aside. Chop the skins in a food processor, chopper, or blender and add ½ cup water; cook the mixture of skins and water gently on low heat for about 20 minutes.

Meanwhile, in another pot, cook the now-skinless grapes until they are soft and can be pushed through a sieve or fine-mesh strainer to remove the seeds. Work in batches when straining to get as much of the pulp as you can.

Combine the grape pulp, skins, and sugar and bring to a boil, following the directions in "How To Make Jam Without Added Pectin."

Peach Jam

- 2 quarts peeled and crushed peaches
- ½ cup water
- 6 cups sugar

Preparing

In a large pot, combine the peaches and water and cook gently for 10 minutes. (The softened fruit is easier to crush.) Add sugar and then follow the directions in "How To Make Jam Without Added Pectin."

Pineapple Jam

- 2 quarts finely chopped pineapple (peeled and cored)
- 5 cups sugar
- 1 lemon, thinly sliced and seeded
- 2 cups water

Preparing

In a large pot, combine all ingredients and bring to a boil, following directions in "How To Make Jam Without Added Pectin."

Strawberry Jam

- 2 quarts crushed strawberries
- 6 cups sugar

Preparing

In a large pot, combine strawberries and sugar and then bring to a boil, following the directions in "How To Make Jam Without Added Pectin."

How To Make Jam With Added Pectin

First of all, a note about packaged pectin: There is powdered pectin and liquid pectin. Powdered pectin has a longer shelf life, so if you buy a quantity of pectin when it comes on sale, powdered will last longer in your pantry. Just be sure to check the "use by" date because pectin does lose its jelling ability over time. Also, in general, powdered pectin is mixed with the unheated crushed fruit and liquid pectin is added to the cooked fruit and sugar mixture immediately after it is taken off the heat. Cooking time is the same for both products—4 minutes at a full rolling boil while stirring constantly.

Your results will be more consistent when you use pectin in your jam recipes, although there is always the chance that you will have a set failure.

When that happens, call it syrup and use it on pancakes or ice cream. It will still taste good!

Directions

- Fill your water-bath canner halfway with water and set the heat on low to bring the water to a simmer.

- Wash and sterilize your jars and keep them hot until you need them, either in your heated dishwasher or by standing them up in your clean sink or a large pot and pouring boiling water over them to cover. When ready to use, make sure you drain the jars well before filling them with the jam.

- Put the screw bands and lids in a pot and cover with water. Bring water to a simmer— don't boil!—and leave them there until ready to use.

- Prepare the fruit. A potato masher works very well for crushing most fruits. The goal is to have very small bits of crushed fruit as well as the juice that's released during crushing without pureeing.

- Using a liquid measuring container, measure out the exact amount of prepared fruit and put it in a very large pot (at least 6 to 8 quarts). Stir in lemon juice or water if the recipe calls for it.

- If you are using powdered pectin, stir it into the crushed fruit now. If using liquid pectin, you will add it after the cooking is complete.

- Measure out the sugar that you will be using and set it aside for now.

- Bring mixture to a full rolling boil on high heat while stirring constantly.

- Quickly stir in the sugar and return to a full rolling boil. Boil for 4 minutes, stirring constantly.

- Remove from heat. If using liquid pectin, stir it in now.

- Allow the jam to settle for 4 to 5 minutes, stirring occasionally so the fruit doesn't float on top of the liquid. Skim off any foam using a metal spoon; this will make your jam prettier in the jar.

- Quickly ladle the jam into your clean, hot jars, filling to within ⅛ inch of the top.
- Wipe the jar rims and threads using a wet paper towel or cloth and cover with the two-piece lids, screwing the bands on tight.
- Place the jars in the canner, making sure there is a rack on the bottom of the canner to lift the jars off the floor of the pot. Water must cover the tops of the jars by 1 to 2 inches; add very hot water if needed.
- Cover canner and bring the water to a boil.

Process jams as follows;

Altitude in Feet	Processing Time
0 – 1,000	10 minutes
1,001 – 3,000	15 minutes
3,001 – 6,000	20 minutes
6,001 – 8,000	25 minutes
8,001 – 10,000	30 minutes

When the processing time is complete, remove the jars from the canner and set on a folded towel or a board to cool completely. After the jars are completely cooled, check to make sure a seal was formed: the center of the lid should be down, and when you press the lid with your finger there should be no movement in the lid and it should not spring back up when pressed. If a jar didn't seal properly, it will need to be refrigerated and used within about 3 weeks.

Let the jars of jam stand at room temperature for 24 hours and then remove the screw bands. Check again to see that a proper seal was made and wipe down the lids and jars before storing. Some jams will take about 2 weeks to become fully set, but you can use it immediately if you wish.

Jam Recipes With Pectin

Apricot Jam With Powdered Pectin

- 5 cups finely chopped or crushed apricots that have been pitted; leave skins on ½ cup lemon juice
- 1 package powdered pectin
- 8 cups sugar

Preparing

Follow the Directions for "How To Make Jam With Added Pectin" for processing directions. Makes about 5 pints.

Blackberry Jam With Liquid Pectin

- 4 cups crushed blackberries
- ¼ cup lemon juice
- 7 cups sugar
- 1 pouch liquid pectin

Preparing

Crush berries and sieve about half of the pulp to remove some of the seeds if you desire. Follow the Directions for "How To Make Jam With Added Pectin" for processing; remember not to add the liquid pectin until after the cooking is complete. Makes about 4 pints.

Blackberry Jam With Powdered Pectin

- 6 cups crushed blackberries
- 1 package powdered pectin
- ¼ cup lemon juice

- 8½ cups sugar

Preparing

Crush berries and sieve about half of the pulp to remove some of the seeds if you desire. Follow the Directions for "How To Make Jam With Added Pectin" for processing. Makes about 6 pints.

Blueberry Jam With Powdered Pectin

- 3¾ cups crushed blueberries
- 1 package powdered pectin
- ¼ cup lemon juice
- 1 cup water
- 6 cups sugar

Preparing

Follow the Directions for "How To Make Jam With Added Pectin" for processing. Makes about 4 pints

Blueberry/Raspberry Jam with Powdered Pectin

- 3 cups blueberries

- 3 cups raspberries
- ¼ cup lemon juice
- 1 box powdered pectin
- 7 cups sugar

Preparing

Follow the Directions for "How To Make Jam With Added Pectin" for processing. Makes about 6 pints

(Sour Or Ground) Cherry Jam With Liquid Pectin

- 4½ cups ground cherries or pitted sour cherries, finely chopped and stems removed
- ¼ cup lemon juice
- 7 cups sugar
- 2 pouches liquid pectin

Preparing

Follow the Directions for "How To Make Jam With Added Pectin" for processing; remember not to add the liquid pectin until after the cooking is complete. Makes about 4 pints.

(Sour Or Ground) Cherry Jam With Powdered Pectin

- 4 cups ground cherries or pitted sour cherries, finely chopped and stems removed
- ¼ cup lemon juice
- 1 package powdered pectin
- 5 cups sugar

Preparing

Follow the Directions for "How To Make Jam With Added Pectin" for processing. Makes about 3 pints

(Sweet) Cherry Jam With Powdered Pectin

- 3 cups finely chopped sweet cherries
- ½ cup lemon juice
- 4½ cups sugar

Preparing

Follow the Directions for "How To Make Jam With Added Pectin" for processing. Makes about 2½ pints.

Fig Jam With Liquid Pectin

- 4 cups crushed figs, with stem ends cut away
- ½ cup lemon juice
- 7½ cups sugar
- 1 pouch liquid pectin

Preparing

Follow the Directions for "How To Make Jam With Added Pectin" for processing; remember not to add the liquid pectin until after the cooking is complete. Makes about 4 pints.

Nectarine Jam With Powdered Pectin

- 5 cups nectarines, peeled, pitted, and finely chopped or crushed
- ½ cup lemon juice
- 1 package powdered pectin
- 7 cups sugar

Preparing

Follow the Directions for "How To Make Jam With Added Pectin" for processing. Makes about 4½ pints.

Peach Jam With Liquid Pectin

- 4½ cups peeled, pitted, and crushed peaches
- ¼ cup lemon juice
- 7 cups sugar
- 1 to 2 oz. finely chopped candied ginger (optional)
- 1 pouch liquid pectin

Preparing

Follow the Directions for "How To Make Jam With Added Pectin" for processing; remember not to add the liquid pectin until after the cooking is complete. Makes about 4 pints.

Peach Jam With Powdered Pectin

- 3¾ cups peeled, pitted, and crushed peaches

- ¼ cup lemon juice
- 1 package powdered pectin
- 5 cups sugar

Preparing

Follow the Directions for "How To Make Jam With Added Pectin" for processing. Makes about 3 pints

Pear Jam With Liquid Pectin

- 4 cups peeled, cored, and finely chopped pears
- ¼ cup lemon juice
- 7 cups sugar
- 2 pouches liquid pectin

Preparing

Follow the Directions for "How To Make Jam With Added Pectin" for processing; remember not to add the liquid pectin until after the cooking is complete. Makes about 4 pints.

Pear Jam With Powdered Pectin

- 4 cups peeled, cored, and finely chopped pears
- ¼ cup lemon juice
- 1 package powdered pectin
- 8½ cups sugar

Preparing

Follow the Directions for "How To Make Jam With Added Pectin" for processing. Makes about 3½ pints.

Pineapple Jam With Liquid Pectin

- 1 20-ounce can crushed pineapple
- 3 T. lemon juice
- 3¼ cups sugar
- 1 pouch liquid pectin

Preparing

Follow the Directions for "How To Make Jam With Added Pectin" for processing; remember not to add the liquid pectin until after the cooking is complete. Makes about 2 pints.

Plum Jam With Liquid Pectin

- 4½ cups pitted and crushed or finely chopped plums
- ¼ cup lemon juice
- 7½ cups sugar
- 1 pouch liquid pectin

Preparing

Follow the Directions for "How To Make Jam With Added Pectin" for processing; remember not to add the liquid pectin until after the cooking is complete. Makes about 4 pints.

Plum Jam With Powdered Pectin

- 6 cups pitted and crushed or finely chopped plums
- ¼ cup lemon juice
- 1 package powdered pectin
- 8 cups sugar

Preparing

Follow the Directions for "How To Make Jam With Added Pectin" for processing. Makes about 4½ pints.

Rhubarb Jam With Powdered Pectin

- 6 cups prepared rhubarb (see directions below)
- 1 package powdered pectin
- 8½ cups sugar

Preparing

To prepare rhubarb: Cut about 4 pounds of red-stalk rhubarb into half-inch pieces. Add 2¼ cups water and ¼ cup lemon juice and bring to a boil. Simmer gently, covered, until very soft, stirring occasionally. Measure out 6 cups and proceed with recipe.

Follow the Directions for "How To Make Jam With Added Pectin" for processing. Makes about 5 pints.

Rhubarb/Strawberry Jam With Liquid Pectin

- 1 cup prepared rhubarb (see directions below)

- 2½ cups crushed strawberries
- 6½ cups sugar
- 1 pouch liquid pectin

Preparing

To prepare rhubarb: Cut about 1 pound of red-stalk rhubarb into half-inch pieces. Add ¼ cup water and 3 tablespoons lemon juice and bring to a boil. Simmer gently, covered, until very soft, stirring occasionally. Measure out 1 cup and proceed with recipe.

Follow the Directions for "How To Make Jam With Added Pectin" for processing; remember not to add the liquid pectin until after the cooking is complete. Makes about 3½ pints.

Strawberry Jam With Liquid Pectin

- 4 cups crushed strawberries
- ¼ cup lemon juice
- 7 cups sugar
- 1 pouch liquid pectin

Preparing

Follow the Directions for "How To Make Jam With Added Pectin" for processing; remember not to add the liquid pectin until after the cooking is complete. Makes about 4 pints.

Strawberry Jam With Powdered Pectin

- 5½ cups crushed strawberries
- ¼ cup lemon juice
- 1 package powdered pectin
- 8 cups sugar

Preparing

Follow the Directions for "How To Make Jam With Added Pectin" for processing. Makes about 5 pints.

Jellies

Many folks make a batch or two of jelly every year, even if they never can anything else. Jelly is a great introduction to the canning process and doesn't require a lot of time if you buy your juice instead of extracting it from the fruit itself. Just make sure that if you purchase juice to turn into jelly it's 100 percent juice with nothing added, such as sugar or corn syrup. I almost always buy grape juice for jelly-making, and more recently I've turned purchased bottles of pomegranate, black cherry, and raspberry juice into jelly as well. There are also some mixed juices available these days that would be interesting to turn into jelly. Why not try something like blueberry/raspberry or cranberry/apple? Really, the flavor variations you can dream up are almost limitless. And another plus for using purchased juice is that you are free to whip up a batch of jelly any time of the year—no need to wait until the fruit is ripe in summer.

How To Prepare The Fruit And Extract The Juice

- Prepare the fruit. Wash the fruit by running cold water over it or else by filling a sink or large container several times with cold water and immersing and then lifting the fruit out each time. You don't want to allow the fruit to sit in the water for very long. The method differs for extracting the juice depending on the kinds of fruit you are processing. Juicy berries can be crushed and the juice extracted without heating, but firm fruit needs to be heated in order to soften it and start the flow of juice, and usually some water is added when the fruit is heated.

- Extract the juice. Once the fruit has been prepared, it's time to extract the juice from the pulp. Put the prepared fruit in a fruit press or strainer, jelly bag (dampen the bag before adding the fruit pulp), or a double thickness of dampened cheesecloth. Allow the fruit to drip, collecting the juice as it does so.

If you let the fruit drip without pressing it or twisting the bag, you will end up with very clear juice, which makes the prettiest jelly. However, it also yields the least amount of juice, so you may want to twist the bag of fruit tightly or squeeze and press the bag in order to render out the most juice that you can. If you decide to use a fruit press or strainer you will probably want to strain the juice one more time—this time using a double thickness of dampened cheesecloth and allowing the juice to run through the material without squeezing or twisting. This will clear the juice perfectly.

How To Make Jelly With Added Pectin

As we learned in the previous section on making jam, pectin comes in two forms: powdered and liquid. Powdered pectin is mixed with the unheated fruit juice while liquid pectin is added to the boiling juice and sugar mixture. The boiling time is the same using either type of pectin—2 minutes at a full rolling boil (a boil that can't be stirred down).

Because jelly must be firm enough to hold its shape when cut, pectin is of great value in ensuring a good set. It is possible to make jelly without added pectin just like pioneer women did, but since we are fortunate to have readily available packaged pectin, it seems a shame to not take advantage of it. So in the recipes that follow you will have a choice between powdered or liquid pectin in each.

Directions

- Fill your water-bath canner halfway with water and set the heat on low to bring the water to a simmer.

- Wash and sterilize your jars and keep them hot until you need them, either in your heated dishwasher or by standing them up in your clean sink or a large pot and pouring boiling water over them to cover.

When ready to use, make sure you drain the jars well before filling them with the jelly.

- Put the screw bands and lids in a pot and cover with water. Bring water to a simmer—don't boil!—and leave them there until ready to use.

- Prepare the fruit and extract the juice.

- Using a liquid measuring container, measure out the exact amount of prepared fruit juice and put it in a very large pot (at least 6 to 8 quarts). Stir in lemon juice or water if the recipe calls for it.

- If you are using powdered pectin, stir it into the juice now. If using liquid pectin, you will add it after the cooking is complete.

- In a separate bowl, measure out the sugar you will be using and set it aside for now.

- Using high heat, bring mixture to a full rolling boil while stirring constantly.

- Quickly stir in the sugar and return to a full rolling boil. Boil for 2 minutes, stirring constantly.

- Remove from heat. If using liquid pectin, stir it in now.
- Quickly skim off foam and then ladle the jelly into your clean, hot jars, filling to within ⅛ inch of the top.
- Wipe the jar rims and threads using a wet paper towel or cloth and cover with the two-piece lids, screwing the bands on tight.
- Place the jars in the canner, making sure there is a rack on the bottom of the canner to lift the jars off the floor of the pot. Water must cover the tops of the jars by 1 to 2 inches; add very hot water if needed to adequately cover the jar tops.
- Cover canner and bring the water to a boil.

Process jelly as follows:

Altitude in Feet	Processing Time
0 – 1,000	5 minutes
1,001 – 3,000	10 minutes
3,001 – 6,000	15 minutes
6,001 – 8,000	20 minutes
8,001 – 10,000	25 minutes

- When the processing time is complete, remove the jars from the canner and set on a folded towel or a board to cool completely. After the jars are completely cooled, check to make sure a seal was formed: the center of the lid should be down, and when you press the lid with your finger, there should be no movement in the lid and it should not spring back up when pressed. If a jar didn't seal properly, it will need to be refrigerated and used within about 3 weeks.

- Let the jars of jelly stand at room temperature for 24 hours and then remove the screw bands, check again that a proper seal was made, and wipe down the lids and jars before storing.

Single Jelly Recipes

Remember! You can always purchase the juice for the following recipes. Just skip the instructions for extracting the juice from the fruit and go immediately to the jelly-making. It's so easy!

Blackberry Jelly With Liquid Pectin

- 4 cups blackberry juice (from about 3 quarts berries, stems and caps removed)
- 7½ cups sugar
- 2 T. lemon juice
- 2 pouches liquid pectin

Preparing

Crush berries and extract juice, following the instructions in "Preparing Fruit and Extracting the Juice." You can also heat the berries first, if desired.

Follow the "Directions for Making Jelly" for processing; remember not to add the liquid pectin until after the cooking is complete. Makes about 4 pints.

Blackberry Jelly With Powdered Pectin

- 3½ cups blackberry juice (from about 2 to 2½ quarts berries, stems and caps removed)
- 5 cups sugar
- 1 package powdered pectin

- 2 T. lemon juice

Preparing

Crush berries and extract juice, following the instructions in "Preparing Fruit and Extracting the Juice." You can also heat the berries first, if desired.

Follow the "Directions for Making Jelly" for processing; remember not to add the liquid pectin until after the cooking is complete. Makes about 3 pints.

Boysenberry Jelly With Powdered Pectin

- 3½ cups boysenberry juice (from about 3 quarts berries)
- 1 package powdered pectin
- 2 T. lemon juice
- 5 cups sugar

Preparing

Crush berries and extract juice, following the instructions in "Preparing Fruit and Extracting the Juice." You can also heat the berries first, if desired.

Follow the "Directions for Making Jelly" for processing; remember not to add the liquid pectin until after the cooking is complete. Makes about 2½ pints.

Cherry Jelly With Liquid Pectin

- 3 cups cherry juice (from about 2 quarts of sour or pie cherries and ½ cup water)
- 7 cups sugar
- 2 pouches liquid pectin

Preparing

Stem cherries; no need to pit them. Crush cherries and place in large pot. Add the water, cover, and bring to a boil on high heat. Reduce the heat and simmer for about 10 minutes before extracting the juice, following the instructions in "Preparing Fruit and Extracting the Juice."

Follow the "Directions for Making Jelly" for processing; remember not to add the liquid pectin until after the cooking is complete. Makes about 4 pints.

Cherry Jelly With Powdered Pectin

- 3½ cups cherry juice (from about 2 quarts of sour or pie cherries and ½ cup water)
- 1 package powdered pectin
- 4½ cups sugar

Preparing

Stem cherries; no need to pit them. Crush cherries and place in large pot. Add the water, cover, and bring to a boil on high heat. Reduce the heat and simmer for about 10 minutes before extracting the juice, following the instructions in "Preparing Fruit and Extracting the Juice."

Follow the "Directions for Making Jelly" for processing. Makes about 3 pints.

Currant Jelly With Liquid Pectin

- 5 cups red currant juice (from about 5 pounds of fruit)

- 7 cups sugar
- 1 pouch liquid pectin

Preparing

Crush currants and then heat, if desired, to help extract the juice, following the instructions in "Preparing Fruit and Extracting the Juice."

Follow the "Directions for Making Jelly" for processing; remember not to add the liquid pectin until after the cooking is complete. Makes about 4 pints.

Elderberry Jelly With Liquid Pectin

- 4 cups elderberry juice (from about 3 quarts berries, stems removed)
- 7½ cups sugar
- 2 T. lemon juice
- 2 pouches liquid pectin

Preparing

Heat berries before crushing, being careful not to scorch them. Crush berries and extract juice, following the instructions in "Preparing Fruit and Extracting the Juice."

Follow the "Directions for Making Jelly" for processing; remember not to add the liquid pectin until after the cooking is complete. Makes about 4 pints.

Elderberry Jelly With Powdered Pectin

- 3½ cups elderberry juice (from about 2½ quarts berries, stems removed)
- 6 cups sugar
- 1 package powdered pectin
- 2 T. lemon juice

Preparing

Heat berries before crushing, being careful not to scorch them. Crush berries and extract juice, following the instructions in "Preparing Fruit and Extracting the Juice."

Follow the "Directions for Making Jelly" for processing. Makes about 3 pints

Grape Jelly With Liquid Pectin

- 4 cups grape juice (from about 3½ pounds Concord grapes and ½ cup water)
- 7 cups sugar
- 1 pouch liquid pectino

Preparing

Stem and then crush grapes. In a large pot, add the grapes and water, cover, and bring to a boil on high heat. Reduce heat and simmer for about 10 minutes. Extract the juice, following the instructions in "Preparing Fruit and Extracting the Juice."

Follow the "Directions for Making Jelly" for processing; remember not to add the liquid pectin until after the cooking is complete. Makes about 4½ pints.

Grape Jelly With Powdered Pectin

- 5 cups grape juice (from about 3½ pounds Concord grapes and 1 cup water)
- 1 package powdered pectin
- 7 cups sugar

Preparing

Stem and then crush grapes. In a large pot, add the grapes and water, cover, and bring to a boil on high heat. Reduce heat and simmer for about 10 minutes. Extract the juice, following the instructions in "Preparing Fruit and Extracting the Juice."

Follow the "Directions for Making Jelly" for processing. Makes about 5 pints.

Mint Jelly With Liquid Pectin

- 1 cup chopped mint leaves and tender stems, packed tightly to measure
- 1 cup water
- ½ cup apple cider vinegar 3½ cups sugar
- 5 drops green food coloring
- 1 pouch liquid pectin

Preparing

Wash and prepare mint leaves. Measure mint into a large pot. Add vinegar, water, and sugar; stir well. On high heat and stirring constantly, bring mixture to a full rolling boil. Add food coloring and pectin; return to a full rolling boil and boil hard for 30 seconds.

Remove from heat and working quickly, skim and then strain jelly through two thicknesses of dampened cheesecloth. Pour strained jelly into jars and process, following the "Directions for Making Jelly". Makes about 2 pints.

Pepper Jelly With Powdered Pectin

- 3 cups prepared pepper juice (from about 1 lb. hot peppers, or a mix of hot and bell peppers, including the vinegar and water used to prepare the juice; see below)
- 1 package powdered pectin
- 4 cups sugar
- 3 to 5 drops green or red food coloring, depending on the color of the juice (optional)

Preparing

Stem peppers and chop, discarding seeds. Finely chop or grind peppers (you can pulse in a food processor or Vitamix) and measure 2 cups into a large pot. Add 2 cups water and 1 cup apple cider vinegar.

Bring to a boil; reduce heat, cover, and simmer for about 15 minutes. You can use the juice including the bits of ground peppers or else strain the juice through several layers of dampened cheesecloth. Follow the "Directions for Making Jelly" for processing. Makes about 2½ pints.

Plum Jelly With Liquid Pectin

- 4 cups plum juice (from about 4½ pounds plums and ½ cup water)
- 7½ cups sugar
- 1 pouch liquid pectin

Preparing

Cut plums into pieces; no need to peel or pit them. Crush the chunks of plums, add the water, cover, and bring to a boil over high heat. Reduce the heat and simmer for 10 minutes to extract the juice, following the instructions in "Preparing Fruit and Extracting the Juice."

Follow the "Directions for Making Jelly" for processing; remember not to add the liquid pectin until after the cooking is complete. Makes about 4 pints.

Plum Jelly With Powdered Pectin

- 5 cups plum juice (from about 4½ pounds plums and 1 cup water)
- 1 package powdered pectin
- 7 cups sugar

Preparing

Cut plums into pieces; no need to peel or pit them. Crush the chunks of plums, add the water, cover, and bring to a boil over high heat. Reduce the heat and simmer for 10 minutes to extract the juice, following the instructions in "Preparing Fruit and Extracting the Juice."

Follow the "Directions for Making Jelly" for processing. Makes about 3½ to 4 pints.

Pomegranate Jelly With Powdered Pectin

- 3½ cups pomegranate juice (from about 10 pomegranates)
- 1 package powdered pectin
- 5 cups sugar

Preparing

If you are ever going to spring for store-bought juice, this is the recipe you want to purchase ready-made juice for. But if you choose to extract the juice from fresh pomegranates, first cut the pomegranates in half and then use a juice reamer (such as you use to juice a lemon or orange) to crush the berries and release the juice. Strain the juice through several layers of dampened cheesecloth, measure out 3½ cups, and proceed.

Follow the "Directions for Making Jelly" for processing. Makes about 3 pints

Raspberry Jelly With Powdered Pectin

- 4 cups raspberry juice (from about 3 quarts berries)

- 1 package powdered pectin
- 5 cups sugar

Preparing

Crush berries and extract juice, following the instructions in "Preparing Fruit and Extracting the Juice." You can also heat the berries first, if desired.

Follow the "Directions for Making Jelly" for processing. Makes about 3 pints.

Strawberry Jelly With Liquid Pectin

- 4 cups strawberry juice (from about 3 quarts berries, stems and caps removed)
- 7½ cups sugar
- 2 T. lemon juice
- 2 pouches liquid pectin

Preparing

Crush berries and extract juice, following the instructions in "Preparing Fruit and Extracting the Juice." You can also heat the berries first, if desired.

Follow the "Directions for Making Jelly" for processing; remember not to add the liquid pectin until after the cooking is complete. Makes about 4 pints.

Strawberry Jelly With Powdered Pectin

- 3½ cups strawberry juice (from about 2½ quarts berries, stems and caps removed)
- 4½ cups sugar
- 1 package powdered pectin
- 2 T. lemon juice

Preparing

Crush berries and extract juice, following the instructions in "Preparing Fruit and Extracting the Juice." You can also heat the berries first, if desired.

Follow the "Step-by-Step Directions for Making Jelly" for processing. Makes about 3 pints.

Chapter 7: Pickles & Sauerkraut

There is an enduring myth that Amish meals always include "seven sweets and seven sours." While this isn't accurate, it is true that Amish folks love to serve pickled foods to round out their meals and help fill up hungry eaters.

Pickling is one of the oldest methods for preserving food, and in many kitchens you'll find cooks who have used a particular pickle recipe for many years and passed that favorite recipe down to the next generation. Now, thanks to modern testing and research, you can analyze these older recipes and decide if they are truly safe or if you will need to make changes to ensure that safety. Pickling prevents spoilage because the acidity of the canned food is high enough that harmful bacteria like clostridium botulinum can't grow. Correctly processing your pickled food prevents the growth of those harmful bacteria.

There are two types of pickles:

Brined or fermented pickles require several weeks of curing at room temperature, during which time the food changes color and flavor and lactic acid is produced, preventing spoilage.

Quick or unfermented pickles are made in one or two days by adding acid in the form of 5% vinegar. The amount of vinegar used is critical to your success and the safety of the finished product, and this is the area where that favorite old-time recipe you like to use may need adjusting.

Tips for Pickling Food Safely

- Always use 5% vinegar, either distilled white or cider. White vinegar has a tart taste and is most often used with light-colored vegetables while cider vinegar has a milder flavor. Unless you have tested the acid level in your homemade vinegar and know it's 5%, you're better off using store-bought.

- Quick or unfermented pickles must have at least as much vinegar as water to be considered safe. An adequate amount of vinegar is the single most important ingredient when making quick pickles. If you find the taste too tart, don't reduce the amount of vinegar used—try adding a bit of sugar instead.

- Brined or fermented pickles (including sauerkraut) must include salt. During the fermenting process, additional salt is sometimes added over a period of several weeks. Several times each week you must check the surface of the fermenting brine and remove any scum that accumulates.

- If you use lime as a firming agent, use only food-grade lime and rinse the food well before processing.

- Quick pickles are processed as soon as they are made while brined pickles must not be processed until they have a sour taste.

Brined / Fermented Pickles Containers

You will need to select a fermenting container, which should be a stoneware crock, glass jar, or food-grade plastic container. A one-gallon container is adequate to brine about 5 pounds of vegetables; you can use quart or half-gallon jars for making sauerkraut, but you might experience more spoilage with them, so it's better to stick with at least a gallon size. If you are brining large quantities of food, do not use a garbage can or any other container that isn't expressly made for contact with food. Also, during the entire process, do not use utensils that consist of zinc, copper, brass, galvanized metal, or iron as these metals may react with the acid or salt and affect the quality, color, and safety of the pickles.

Make sure all of the equipment you use has been thoroughly cleaned.

Weights: A weight is needed to keep the food under the brine solution while the fermenting process takes place. You can use a plate (such as a dinner plate or pie pan) that is slightly smaller than the container opening. On top of this plate, stand 2 or 3 quart jars filled with water and tightly covered so even if they tip, there is no leakage into the fermenting crock. You can also use large food-grade plastic bags (quart or gallon freezer bags work well) filled with a solution of 1½ tablespoons salt for every 1 quart water; make sure the bags are completely closed and then double bag them for added measure. Whichever type of weight you use, you will want to adjust the amount of water used (or brine if using plastic bags) in order to provide just enough weight to keep the food under the brine.

When fermenting, make sure to keep the food 1 to 2 inches under the brine.

After weighting down the food, cover the container opening with a clean, heavy bath towel to prevent contamination from insects and molds.

Water: Soft water makes the best brine for pickles. But if you have hard water, you can boil your water and then let it set in the covered container undisturbed for 24 hours. Now skim off any scum that appears across the top and then carefully ladle out the water without disturbing the sediment that might have collected at the bottom of the pot.

Note: You can safely use table salt, but there are additives that might turn your brine cloudy—it's better to use pickling or canning salt. Also, never use reduced-sodium, flake, sea, sour, or rock salt. Do not use salt substitutes.

Brined Pickle & Sauerkraut Recipes

When making the following recipes, take care to accurately measure the ingredients. And except for any optional ingredients, don't deviate from the recipe. If you follow these guidelines, you are sure to have success with great tasting, old-fashioned brined pickles and sauerkraut. Yum!

Dill Pickles (Brined)

Choose tender, ripe cucumbers that do not have any blemishes. Begin the brining process as soon after harvesting as possible—within 24 hours is best.

Carefully wash cucumbers: Using a soft brush or cloth, gently scrub the cukes so as to remove any clinging soil or debris, which can cause spoilage. Rinse the cucumbers several times in fresh, cool water. Cut -inch off of the blossom ends. You can cut off the stem ends or leave ¼-inch of the stem attached if you prefer.

Next, you will fill your crock or other brining container. The following quantities will fill a gallon container. Adjust the amounts depending on the container size:

- 4 lbs. pickling cucumbers of uniform size
- 4 to 5 heads fresh or dry dill weed or 2 T. dill seed 2 cloves garlic (optional)
- 2 dried red peppers (optional)
- 2 tsp. whole mixed pickling spices
- ½ cup salt
- ¼ cup 5% vinegar
- 8 cups water

Preparing

Place half of the dill and other spices (do not add the salt, vinegar, or water yet) into the bottom of the container. Add cucumbers and the remaining dill and spices.

Dissolve the salt into the vinegar and water and pour over cucumbers. Place the weight over the top, making sure that the cukes are kept 1 to 2 inches under the brine solution. Cover with a heavy towel to keep insects from getting into the brine.

Find a place where the temperature is between 55 and 75 degrees. Pickles stored at 70 to 75 degrees will take about 3 to 4 weeks to fully ferment. If the temperature drops to between 55 and 65 degrees, fermentation will take 5 to 6 weeks. If the temperature gets higher than 80 degrees the pickles will become too soft, and if the temperature falls below 55 degrees fermentation may not take place.

Check the container several times a week and remove any scum that appears on the surface. If the pickles become soft or slimy, or if they develop an unpleasant odor, discard them and start over. The fermentation process should begin in 2 to 3 days. Bubbles will appear and the color of the cucumbers will begin to change. When the pickles are fully fermented and have the characteristic sour taste, you can store them in the original container for 4 to 6 months in the refrigerator; just remember to keep regularly removing any surface scum that appears. But a better way to store your fermented pickles is to can them.

Canning Fermented Pickles

Pour off the brine from your fully fermented pickles into a large pot and heat slowly to a boil. Simmer for 5 minutes. Filter the brine through paper coffee filters to reduce cloudiness, if desired. Fill pint or quart jars with the pickles and hot brine, leaving ½-inch headspace. Follow the directions in chapter 3, "Water-Bath Canning," process the pickles as follows:

Process quarts for 15 minutes at 0 to 1,000 feet altitude; 20 minutes at 1,001 to

6,000 feet altitude; 25 minutes above 6,000 feet.
Process pints for 10 minutes at 0 to 1,000 feet altitude; 15 minutes at 1,001 to
6,000 feet altitude; 20 minutes above 6,000 feet.
Alternately, you can process the jars using the "Lower-Temperature Pasteurization Process" found at the end of this chapter.

Sauerkraut

- 5 lbs. cabbage per 1 gallon
- 3 T. canning or pickling salt

Preparing

Choose cabbages with firm heads. Use within 48 hours of harvest for best quality. Discard outer leaves and rinse heads under cold running water; drain. Cut heads into quarters and remove cores.
Regardless of how much cabbage you have to process, only work with 5 pounds at a time. Shred or slice cabbage very thin (about the thickness of a quarter). Put the shredded cabbage into the fermentation container and add 3 tablespoons salt. Mix thoroughly, using your (clean!) hands.

Once the salt and cabbage have been mixed, you now want to pack the cabbage. Pack by pushing hard on the cabbage with your fist and keep mixing and packing until the juices from the cabbage have been released. Repeat the shredding, salting, and packing until all of the cabbage is in the container. Be sure the container is deep enough that there are at least 4 to 5 inches of open container above the top level of the cabbage. If the released juice doesn't cover the cabbage (you might have to press down a bit on the top because the cabbage will tend to float) you will need to add boiled and cooled brine, which is made with 1½ tablespoons of salt per quart of water.

Add weights and then cover the container with a clean towel. If you use a plate and weights, you will need to inspect the kraut 2 or 3 times each week and remove any scum that appears on the surface. If you use plastic bags filled with salt water, leave the container undisturbed until fermentation is complete—when bubbling stops. If your kraut is in a 1-gallon container, fermentation usually takes place within 10 to 14 days. For larger containers, fermentation is complete in 3 to 4 weeks if kept between 70 and 75 degrees. At 60 degrees, fermentation

can take 5 to 6 weeks.

You can keep fully fermented sauerkraut in the refrigerator tightly covered for several months or can the kraut for longer storage as follows:

Hot Pack

In a large pot, slowly heat kraut and brining liquid to a boil, stirring frequently. Firmly pack hot kraut into hot jars, leaving half an inch of headspace. Following the directions in chapter 3, "Water-Bath Canning" process the sauerkraut as follows:

Process quarts for 15 minutes at 0 to 1,000 feet altitude; 20 minutes at 1,001 to 6,000 feet altitude; 25 minutes above 6,000 feet.

Process pints for 10 minutes at 0 to 1,000 feet altitude; 15 minutes at 1,001 to 6,000 feet altitude; 20 minutes above 6,000 feet.

Raw Pack

Fill jars firmly with sauerkraut and brining liquid, leaving ½-inch headspace. Following the directions in chapter 3, "Water-Bath Canning Guide," process the sauerkraut as follows:

- Process quarts for 25 minutes at 0 to 1,000 feet altitude; 30 minutes at 1,001 to 3,000 feet altitude; 35 minutes at 3,001 to 6,000 feet altitude; 40 minutes above 6,000 feet.

- Process pints for 20 minutes at 0 to 1,000 feet altitude; 25 minutes at 1,001 to 3,000 feet altitude; 30 minutes at 3,001 to 6,000 feet altitude; 35 minutes above 6,000 feet.

Alternately, you can process the jars using the "Lower-Temperature Pasteurization Process" found at the end of this chapter.

Fresh-Pack / Quick Pickles Recipes

Fresh-packed, or "quick," pickle recipes are easily made in only one or two days; some are brined for several hours or overnight and then drained and processed with vinegar and spices, while some recipes call for immediate processing. Fruit pickles are prepared by heating the fruit in syrup to which either lemon juice or vinegar has been added. Because quick pickles use acid in the form of added vinegar to prevent bacterial growth, you must carefully measure the vinegar amounts used in the following recipes to ensure that your finished product will be safe.

Fresh-pack pickles don't develop flavor from a long fermentation period, so it's a good idea to allow the jars of processed food to remain unopened for several weeks in order for the flavors to fully develop.

Pickled Asparagus

- 8 pints fresh asparagus spears
- 6 cups water
- 6 cups 5% vinegar
- 6 T. salt
- 2 tsp. pickling spices with no cloves, tied into a clean, thin white bag (you can

remove the cloves if your pickling spice mix contains them)

- Garlic, 1 clove per jar

Preparing

Wash asparagus and cut the stem ends enough so spears fit into pint or quart jars.

Combine water, vinegar, salt, and pickling spice bag. Heat mixture to boiling and then remove spice bag.

Put 1 clove garlic into each jar; pack asparagus into jars, tip ends down for easier removal later. Cover with boiling vinegar solution, leaving ½-inch headspace. Following the directions in chapter 3, "Water-Bath Canning Guide," process the pickled asparagus as follows: Process pints or quarts for 10 minutes at 0 to 1,000 feet altitude; 15 minutes at 1,001 to 6,000 feet altitude; 20 minutes above 6,000 feet.

Alternatively, you can process the jars using the "Lower-Temperature Pasteurization Process" found at the end of this chapter.

Makes about 8 pints.

Pickled Dilly Beans

- 4 lbs. fresh tender green or yellow beans
- 8 to 16 heads fresh dill
- 8 cloves garlic
- ½ cup pickling or canning salt
- 4 cups 5% vinegar
- 4 cups water
- 1 tsp. hot red pepper flakes (optional)

Preparing

Wash and trim ends of beans.

In each pint jar, place 1 or 2 dill heads and 1 clove garlic. Pack jars (pints only) with beans, standing them upright; trim beans if necessary to ensure proper fit, leaving half an inch of headspace.

Combine salt, vinegar, water, and pepper flakes (if using). Bring to a boil. Add hot vinegar solution to beans, leaving ½ inch of headspace. Following the directions in chapter 3, "Water-Bath Canning," process the pickled dilly beans as follows: Process pints for 5 minutes at 0 to 1,000 feet altitude; 10 minutes at 1,001 to 6,000 feet altitude; 15 minutes above 6,000 feet.

Alternatively, you can process the jars using the "Lower-Temperature Pasteurization Process" found at the end of this chapter.

Makes about 8 pints.

Pickled Three-Bean Salad

- 1½ cups fresh green or yellow beans
- 1½ cups canned red kidney beans, drained
- 1 cup canned garbanzo beans, drained
- ½ cup onion, thinly sliced
- ½ cup celery, trimmed and thinly sliced
- ½ cup sliced green peppers
- ½ cup 5% vinegar
- ¼ cup bottled lemon juice
- ¾ cup sugar
- 1¼ cups water
- ¼ cup oil
- ½ tsp. pickling or canning salt

Preparing

Wash and snap ends off of fresh beans. Cut into 1- to 2-inch pieces. Blanch 3 minutes and then cool immediately. Rinse kidney beans and drain again. Prepare remainder of vegetables.

In a large pot, combine vinegar, lemon juice, sugar, and water and bring to a boil. Remove from heat. Add oil and salt and mix well. Add vegetables and return to heat; bring to a simmer. Cover and refrigerate for 12 to 14 hours so vegetables have time to marinate.

After marinating, return the pot with vegetables and vinegar solution to the stove and heat the contents to a boil. Fill half-pint or pint jars with vegetables and then ladle hot cooking liquid over the top, leaving ½-inch headspace. Following the directions in chapter 3, "Water-Bath Canning," process the pickled three-bean salad as follows: Process half-pints or pints for 15 minutes at 0 to 1,000 feet altitude; 20 minutes at 1,001 to 6,000 feet altitude; 25 minutes above 6,000 feet.

Alternately, you can process the jars using the "Lower-Temperature Pasteurization Process" found at the end of this chapter.

Makes 5 to 6 half-pints.

Pickled Beets

- 7 lbs. beets, uniform size
- 4 cups 5% vinegar
- 1½ tsp. pickling or canning salt
- 2 cups sugar
- 2 cups water
- 2 cinnamon sticks
- 12 whole cloves
- 4 to 6 small onions (optional)

Preparing

Trim beets ends, leaving 1 inch of stem and roots. Wash thoroughly. Place beets in a large pot and add water to cover. Bring to a boil and boil until beets are tender, about 25 to 30 minutes. Drain and discard cooking liquid.

Cool beets. Trim off roots and stems and slip off skins. Slice into thin slices, about ¼-inch thick. Peel and thinly slice onions.

Combine vinegar, salt, sugar, and 2 cups water. Put spices in a spice or cheesecloth bag and add to vinegar mixture. Bring to a boil. Add beets and onions and simmer 5 minutes. Remove spice bag.

Fill jars with beet mixture, leaving ½-inch headspace. Following the directions in chapter 3, "Water-Bath Canning" process the pickled beets as follows: Process pints or quarts for 30 minutes at 0 to 1,000 feet altitude; 35 minutes at 1,001 to 3,000 feet altitude; 40 minutes at 3,001 to 6,000 feet altitude; 45 minutes above 6,000 feet.

Alternately, you can process the jars using the "Lower-Temperature Pasteurization Process" found at the end of this chapter.

Makes about 8 pints.

Chow Chow

- 1 cup green tomatoes, chopped
- 1 cup bell peppers, chopped
- 1 cup cabbage, chopped
- 1 whole cucumber, chopped
- 1 cup onions, chopped
- 2 quarts water
- ¼ cup salt
- 1 cup carrots, chopped
- 1 cup green beans, chopped

- 2 tsp. mustard seed
- 2 tsp. celery seed
- 2 cups vinegar
- 2 cups sugar

Preparing

Soak tomatoes, peppers, cabbage, cucumber, and onions overnight in water and salt. Drain; rinse and drain again. Cook carrots and green beans for 10 minutes; drain. In a large pot, mix together all ingredients; heat to boiling. Pack hot chow chow into hot pint jars, leaving ¼-inch headspace.

Following the directions in chapter 3, "Water-Bath Canning Guide," process the chow chow as follows: Process pints for 10 minutes at 0 to 1,000 feet altitude; 15 minutes at 1,001 to 6,000 feet altitude; 20 minutes above 6,000 feet.

Makes about 4 pints.

Deluxe Chow Chow

- Vegetables, chunked
- 2 quarts plus 1 pint cauliflower
- 3 pints carrots

- 2 quarts plus 1 pint celery
- 3½ pints green and red peppers
- 2½ pints baby lima beans
- 2 pints sour pickles
- 1 heaping quart onions salt to taste

Syrup

- 4 cups vinegar
- 2 cups cooking liquid from cooked celery
- 5½ lbs. sugar
- ¾ cup prepared mustard
- 3 T. mustard seed
- 2 tsp. turmeric
- 1 tsp. celery seed

Preparing

Dice each vegetable in ½-to 1-inch chunks. Cook each vegetable separately in a pot of boiling water (except for the pickles) just until softened. Season each with salt. Drain and gently mix all vegetables together.

Combine all syrup ingredients in a large pot. Add the mixed vegetables and heat to the boiling point. Pack hot chow chow into hot pint jars, leaving ¼-inch headspace. Following the directions in chapter 3, "Water-Bath Canning: A Step- by-Step Guide," process the chow chow as follows: Process pints for 15 minutes at 0 to 1,000 feet altitude; 20 minutes at 1,001 to 6,000 feet altitude; 25 minutes

above 6,000 feet. Makes about 14 pints.

Pickled Whole Mushrooms

- 7 lbs. small whole fresh button mushrooms (less than 1¼ inch in diameter)
- ½ cup bottled lemon juice
- 2 cups olive oil or salad oil
- 2½ cups 5% vinegar
- 1 T. oregano
- 1 T. basil
- 1 T. pickling or canning salt
- ½ cup finely chopped onion
- ¼ cup pimento, diced
- 2 to 3 cloves garlic, cut in quarters
- 25 black peppercorns

Preparing

Note: Do not use wild-harvested mushrooms.

Wash mushrooms; cut stems, leaving ¼ inch attached to cap. Combine mushrooms, lemon juice, and water to cover in a large pot. Simmer for 5 minutes. Drain mushrooms.

Mix olive oil, vinegar, oregano, basil, and salt in a saucepan. Stir in onions and pimento and heat to boiling, mixing well.

Place ¼ garlic clove and 2 to 3 peppercorns in each half-pint jar. Fill jars with mushrooms and boiling vinegar solution, leaving ½-inch headspace.

Following the directions in chapter 3, "Water-Bath Canning Guide," process the pickled mushrooms as follows: Process half-pints for 20 minutes at 0 to 1,000 feet altitude; 25 minutes at 1,001 to 3,000 feet altitude; 30 minutes at 3,001 to 6,000 feet altitude; 35 minutes above 6,000 feet.

Makes about 9 half-pints.

Pickled Hot Peppers

- 4 lbs. hot peppers, red, green, or yellow (Hungarian, banana, chili, jalapeno, Serrano)
- 3 lbs. sweet red and green peppers, mixed
- 5 cups 5% vinegar
- 1 cup water
- 4 tsp. pickling or canning salt
- 2 T. sugar
- 2 cloves garlic

Preparing

Note: To prevent burns, wear rubber gloves when handling hot peppers and don't touch your face. Wash hands thoroughly when done.

To prepare peppers, first wash them. Cut larger peppers in half or in quarters; small peppers may be left whole but you'll need to make 3 or 4 slits through the skin or else flatten them. Blanch peppers in boiling water to help remove skins, or blister skins by placing peppers in a 400-degree oven or under the broiler for 6 to 8 minutes, turning to get all sides, until skins blister. Cool peppers by placing them in a pan and covering them with a damp towel. After several minutes the pepper skins should peel off easily. Fill half-pint or pint jars with the peppers, leaving ½-inch headspace.

Combine remaining ingredients and bring to a boil; simmer for 10 minutes. Remove garlic. Ladle boiling vinegar solution over peppers, leaving ½-inch headspace. Following the directions in chapter 3, "Water-Bath Canning Guide," process the pickled peppers as follows: Process half-pints and pints for 10 minutes at 0 to 1,000 feet altitude; 15 minutes at 1,001 to 6,000 feet altitude; 20 minutes above 6,000 feet.

Makes about 9 pints.

Bread & Butter Pickles

- 4 lbs. pickling cucumbers, cut into ¼-inch slices
- 2 lbs. onions (about 8 small), thinly sliced
- ⅓ cup pickling or canning salt
- 2 cups sugar

- 2 T. mustard seed
- 2 tsp. turmeric
- 2 tsp. celery seed
- 1 tsp. peppercorns
- 3 cups 5% vinegar

Preparing

Combine cucumber and onion slices in a large bowl, layering with salt. Cover with 2 inches crushed or cubed ice; refrigerate for 3 hours, adding more ice as necessary. Drain, rinse well, and drain again.

Combine remaining ingredients in a large pot; bring to a boil. Add drained cucumbers and onions and return to a boil. Pack hot cucumbers, onions, and vinegar mixture into hot pint or quart jars. Following the directions in chapter 3, "Water-Bath Canning Guide," process the pickles as follows: Process pints or quarts for 10 minutes at 0 to 1,000 feet altitude; 15 minutes at 1,001 to 6,000 feet altitude; 20 minutes above 6,000 feet.

Alternately, you can process the jars using the "Lower-Temperature Pasteurization Process" found at the end of this chapter.

Makes about 7 pints.

Kosher Dill Pickles

- 4 lbs. pickling cucumbers, uniform size
- 14 cloves garlic, peeled and cut in half
- ¼ cup pickling or canning salt
- 2¾ cups 5% vinegar
- 3 cups water
- 14 heads fresh dill
- 28 peppercorns

Preparing

Wash cucumbers and remove blossom end. Remove stem or leave ¼ inch of stem intact. Cut in half lengthwise. Heat garlic, vinegar, and water to boiling.

Into each pint or quart jar put 4 halved garlic cloves. Add the cucumbers, 2 heads dill, and 4 peppercorns. Pour hot vinegar solution over cucumbers, leaving

½-inch headspace.

Following the directions in chapter 3, "Water-Bath Canning Guide," process the pickles as follows: Process quarts for 15 minutes at 0 to 1,000 feet altitude; 20 minutes at 1,001 to 6,000 feet altitude; 25 minutes above 6,000 feet.

Process pints for 10 minutes at 0 to 1,000 feet altitude; 15 minutes at 1,001 to 6,000 feet altitude; 20 minutes above 6,000 feet.

Alternately, you can process the jars using the "Lower-Temperature Pasteurization Process" found at the end of this chapter.

Makes 6 to 7 pints.

Sweet Gherkins

- 7 lbs. tiny pickling cucumbers (1½ inches long or less)
- ½ cup pickling or canning salt
- 6 cups 5% vinegar, divided
- 8 cups sugar, divided
- ¾ tsp. turmeric
- 2 tsp. celery seeds

- 2 tsp. whole mixed pickling spice
- 2 cinnamon sticks
- ½ tsp. fennel (optional)
- ½ tsp. whole allspice (optional)

Preparing

Wash cucumbers. Cut -inch slice off blossom ends and discard; leave ¼ inch of stems attached.

Days 1 and 2: Place cucumbers in a large container and cover with boiling water. Let sit for 6 to 8 hours, drain and cover with 6 quarts of fresh boiling water to which ¼ cup salt has been added. Repeat this process on day 2.

Day 3: Drain and prick cucumbers with a fork. Combine and bring to a boil 3 cups vinegar, 3 cups sugar, and the spices. Pour over cucumbers. Let sit for 6 to 8 hours and drain, saving the pickling liquid. Add another 2 cups each of sugar and vinegar to the pickling liquid and reheat to boiling. Pour over cucumbers.

Day 4: Drain and save pickling liquid. Add another 2 cups sugar and 1 cup vinegar. Heat pickling liquid to boiling and pour over pickles.

Let sit for 6 to 8 hours and drain, saving the pickling liquid. Add 1 cup sugar and heat to boiling. Fill pint jars with pickles and cover with hot pickling liquid, leaving ½-inch headspace. Following the directions in chapter 3, "Water-Bath Canning Guide," process the pickles as follows: Process pints and quarts for 5 minutes at 0 to 1,000 feet altitude; 10 minutes at 1,001 to 6,000 feet altitude; 15 minutes above 6,000 feet. Alternately, you can process the jars using the "Lower-Temperature Pasteurization Process" found at the end of this chapter.

Makes about 6 to 7 pints.

Sweet Pickles

- 4 lbs. pickling cucumbers, uniform size
- 4½ cups sugar
- 3½ cups 5% vinegar
- 2 tsp. celery seed
- 1 T. whole allspice
- 2 T. mustard seed

Preparing

Wash cucumbers. Cut off blossom end and leave ¼ inch of stem at other end. Slice or cut larger cukes into spears. Place cucumbers in a large bowl or pot and sprinkle with ⅓ cup salt, gently mixing to incorporate salt throughout. Cover cucumbers with 2 inches of ice (crushed or cubed) and refrigerate for 3 to 4 hours, adding more ice as needed. Drain well when ready to process.

Combine sugar, vinegar, celery seed, allspice, and mustard seed in a large pot. Heat to boiling.

Hot Pack: Add cucumbers to the vinegar solution and heat slowly until the vinegar solution returns to a boil, stirring occasionally. Fill pint or quart jars with pickles and vinegar solution, leaving ½-inch headspace. Following the directions in chapter 3, "Water-Bath Canning Guide," process the pickles as follows: Process pints or quarts for 5 minutes at 0 to 1,000 feet altitude; 10 minutes at 1,001 to 6,000 feet altitude; 15 minutes above 6,000 feet.

Raw Pack: Fill jars with cucumbers. Ladle hot vinegar solution over cucumbers, leaving ½-inch headspace. Following the directions in chapter 3,

"Water-Bath Canning: A Step-by-Step Guide," process the pickles as follows: Process quarts for 15 minutes at 0 to 1,000 feet altitude; 20 minutes at 1,001 to 6,000 feet altitude; 25 minutes above 6,000 feet.

Process pints for 10 minutes at 0 to 1,000 feet altitude; 15 minutes at 1,001 to 6,000 feet altitude; 20 minutes above 6,000 feet.

Alternately, you can process the jars using the "Lower-Temperature Pasteurization Process" found at the end of this chapter.

Makes about 7 to 9 pints.

Dill Pickle Relish

- 8 lbs. pickling cucumbers
- ½ cup salt
- 2 tsp. turmeric
- 1 quart water
- 1 lb. onions
- ⅓ cup sugar
- 2 T. dill seed

- 1 quart 5% vinegar (white wine vinegar gives a good taste)

Preparing

Wash cucumbers; drain. Finely chop cucumbers; place chopped cucumbers in a bowl and sprinkle with salt and turmeric. Pour water over cucumbers and let set for 2 hours. Drain cucumbers, rinse under cold water, and drain again. Finely chop onions. Combine cucumbers, onions, sugar, dill seed, and vinegar in a large pot; bring to a boil, reduce heat, and simmer for 10 minutes.

Pack hot relish into hot jars, leaving ¼-inch headspace. Following the directions in chapter 3, "Water-Bath Canning Guide," process the relish as follows: Process pints for 15 minutes at 0 to 1,000 feet altitude; 20 minutes at 1,001 to 6,000 feet altitude; 25 minutes above 6,000 feet.

Makes about 7 pints.

Sweet Pickle Relish

- 3 quarts chopped cucumbers

- 3 cups each chopped sweet green and red peppers
- 1 cup chopped onions
- ¾ cup pickling or canning salt
- 4 cups ice
- 8 cups water
- 2 cups sugar
- 4 tsp. each mustard seed, turmeric, whole allspice, and whole cloves
- 6 cups 5% vinegar

Preparing

Put cucumbers, peppers, onions, salt, and ice in water and let set for 4 hours. Drain and re-cover vegetables with fresh ice water for another hour; drain again and put in a large pot.

Combine spices in a spice or cheesecloth bag. Add together sugar, vinegar, and spice bag. Heat to boiling and then pour over vegetables in the pot. Cover and refrigerate for 24 hours.

Remove vegetable mixture from refrigerator and heat to boiling. Ladle hot relish into hot half-pint or pint jars, leaving ½-inch headspace. Following the directions in chapter 3, "Water-Bath Canning Guide," process the relish as follows: Process half-pints and pints for 10 minutes at 0 to 1,000 feet altitude; 15 minutes at 1,001 to 6,000 feet altitude; 20 minutes above 6,000 feet.

Alternately, you can process the jars using the "Lower-Temperature Pasteurization Process" found at the end of this chapter.

Makes about 9 pints.

Watermelon Rind Pickles

- 4 quarts cubed watermelon rind, white portion only (pieces about 1-inch square)
- 1 cup pickling or canning salt
- 3 sticks cinnamon
- 1 T. whole cloves
- 1 T. whole allspice
- ¼ tsp. mustard seed
- 7 cups sugar
- ½ cup thinly sliced lemon
- 2 cups vinegar

Preparing

In a large container, place watermelon rind, salt, and 1 gallon water; stir until salt is dissolved. Place in refrigerator overnight. Drain and rinse.

In a large pot, add watermelon rind and 1 gallon fresh water; gently simmer until rind is tender; drain.

Tie spices in a thin cloth or cheesecloth spice bag. In a large pot, add spice bag, sugar, lemon slices, and vinegar; bring to a boil and then reduce heat and simmer for 10 minutes. Add rinds and continue to simmer until rinds are transparent.

Remove spice bag and pack hot rinds and liquid into hot jars, leaving ¼-inch headspace. Following the directions in chapter 3, "Water-Bath Canning Guide," process the watermelon pickles as follows: Process pints for 10 minutes at 0 to 1,000 feet altitude; 15 minutes at 1,001 to 6,000 feet altitude; 20 minutes above 6,000 feet.

Alternately, you can process the jars using the "Lower-Temperature Pasteurization Process" found at the end of this chapter.

Makes about 6 pints.

Lower-Temperature Pasteurization Technique

An alternative to the common practice of water-bath canning your pickles is pasteurizing them instead. By keeping the temperature lower, your pickles will tend to be crisper than when water-bath canned; however, you must monitor the processing carefully to ensure that the water temperature doesn't go below the safe limits.

Directions

Place your filled jars in a water-bath canner or other very large pot that has been filled halfway with 120°F to 140°F water. Once the jars are all placed, fill the pot with hot water to 1 inch above the top of the jars. Heat the water to 180°F to 185°F, checking the water temperature regularly with a candy or jelly thermometer. Maintain this water temperature for 30 minutes. When processing is complete, remove jars and let set until completely cool before checking seals.

With all that stated, let move to our next chapter, don't forget to leave me your honest review, it goes a long way, thanks

Chapter 8: Tomatoes

Tomatoes deserve a chapter all to themselves because they are such a popular food to preserve and you can use them in so many ways. In fact, gardeners grow more tomatoes than any other vegetable (although technically, tomatoes are considered a fruit), and they are prolific producers. Just a few plants in your garden will mean you must come up with ways to use the abundant harvest besides just eating them fresh, and canning the excess will give you the makings for lots of great meals come winter. Use your surplus tomatoes to make juice, sauce, salsa, canned tomatoes (either crushed, chopped, or whole), catsup, soup, jam, and jelly. Or do like I do and plant extra on purpose so you have plenty to process.

Canning Tomatoes Safely

Up until the 1990s, tomatoes were canned for a relatively short time using the water-bath canning method with no added acidifier. But the USDA said this was no longer safe and issued updated guidelines that specify longer processing times and added acid in the form of lemon juice, citric acid, or vinegar. And while it's true that many people still can tomato products using outdated methods, usually with no problem, it just makes sense to carefully analyze your recipes and make changes according to these new directives so you can guarantee the safety of your food.

Directions

Use an acidifier. Processing times will vary depending on the product you wish to can, but an acidifier must always be used.

For quarts, add 2 tablespoons lemon juice or ½ tsp. citric acid or 4 tablespoons 5% vinegar.

For pints, add 1 tablespoon lemon juice or ¼ tsp. citric acid or 2 tablespoons 5% vinegar.

You can add the acidifier directly to each jar before filling, and you can also add a bit of sugar to taste to offset the acid taste if desired, but this is not necessary. Usually about 2 tsp. of sugar per quart and 1 tsp. per pint is enough to mask the sour flavor.

Cold pack or hot pack. The next thing to consider is whether you will be hot packing or cold packing your tomatoes. Hot packing means that you will partially cook the tomato recipe and then pack the canning jars with the hot food. Cold packing (also known as raw packing) is simply putting raw tomatoes into your jars along with your choice of acidifier and following the processing instructions. Keep these guidelines in mind as you prepare your tomatoes:

- Crushed tomatoes: hot pack only
- Tomato or vegetable juice blend: hot pack only
- Tomato sauce: hot pack only
- Whole or halved tomatoes: raw (cold) pack or hot pack Preparing Tomatoes

Choose ripe or slightly under-ripe tomatoes from vines that are not dead or frost-killed. Wash the tomatoes in cold water to remove dirt and other debris. Remove the skins by dipping the tomatoes in boiling water for about 30 to 60 seconds or until the skins begin to crack and split. Remove them from the boiling water and immediately plunge them into cold water so they are cool enough to handle—the skins should slip right off. You will also want to remove the cores.

Now you are ready to prepare your recipe of choice for canning.

Stewed Tomatoes

- 24 cups tomatoes, chopped
- 2 cups celery, chopped
- 1 cup onion, chopped
- 1 cup green bell pepper, chopped

Preparing

Salt and lemon juice (see below for quantities) Combine tomatoes, celery, onion, and bell pepper in a large pot and simmer for 10 minutes. (Do not add more celery, onion, or green pepper than called for in this recipe; it will make the pH less acidic and not safe for the water-bath canning process.) When packing stewed tomatoes into hot jars, add 1 tsp. salt and 2 tablespoons lemon juice to each quart jar; ½ tsp. salt and 1 tablespoon lemon juice to each pint jar. Pack tomatoes into jars, leaving

½-inch headspace.

Following the instructions for water-bath canning (chapter 3), process for the correct amount of time as follows: Water-Bath Canner

Jar Size	Processing time for 0 – 1,000 feet	Processing time for 1,001 – 3,000 feet	Processing time for 3,001 – 6,000 feet	Processing time above 6,000 feet
Pint	40 minutes	45 minutes	50 minutes	55 minutes
Quart	50 minutes	55 minutes	60 minutes	65 minutes

Tomato Juice—Hot Pack

Quarter or chunk tomatoes and place in large pot. Crush them as they begin to heat up and simmer the mixture for about 5 minutes. Press the softened crushed tomatoes through a sieve or food mill to remove seeds.

Heat the juice again to boiling. Following the instructions for water-bath canning (chapter 3) or pressure canning (chapter 4), fill prepared jars with your acidifier of choice, add salt if desired (1 tsp. per quart or ½ tsp. per pint), and fill with the hot tomato juice, leaving ½-inch headspace.

Process for the correct amount of time as follows:

Water-Bath Canner

Jar Size	Processing time for 0 – 1,000 feet	Processing time for 1,001 – 3,000 feet	Processing time for 3,001 – 6,000 feet	Processing time above 6,000 feet
Pint	35 minutes	40 minutes	45 minutes	50 minutes
Quart	40 minutes	45 minutes	50 minutes	55 minutes

Pressure Canner

Process quarts and pints for 15 minutes as follows: Weighted gauge canner: Process at 10 pounds pressure from sea level to 1,000 feet in altitude; at 15 pounds pressure above 1,000 feet.

Dial gauge canner: Process at 11 pounds pressure from sea level to 2,000 feet in altitude; at 12 pounds pressure from 2,001 to 4,000 feet; at 13 pounds pressure from 4,001 to 6,000 feet; at 14 pounds pressure from 6,001 to 8,000 feet.

Tomato & Vegetable Juice Blend—Hot Pack

Prepare and crush tomatoes. For each canner load of tomato juice (7 quarts, from 20 to 25 pounds of tomatoes), add a maximum of 3 cups of any combination of finely chopped carrots, celery, onions, and peppers. Simmer the tomato/vegetable mixture for 20 minutes, stirring occasionally, and then press hot vegetables through a sieve or food mill. Return tomato/vegetable juice to the pot and heat once more to boiling.

Following the instructions for water-bath canning (chapter 3) or pressure canning (chapter 4), fill prepared jars with your acidifier of choice, add salt to taste, and fill with the hot juice, leaving ½-inch headspace.

Process for the correct amount of time as follows: Water-Bath Canner

Jar Size	Processing time for 0 – 1,000 feet	Processing time for 1,001 – 3,000 feet	Processing time for 3,001 – 6,000 feet	Processing time above 6,000 feet
Pint	35 minutes	40 minutes	45 minutes	50 minutes
Quart	40 minutes	45 minutes	50 minutes	55 minutes

Pressure Canner

Process quarts and pints for 15 minutes as follows: Weighted gauge canner: Process at 10 pounds pressure from sea level to 1,000 feet in altitude; at 15 pounds pressure above 1,000 feet.

Dial gauge canner: Process at 11 pounds pressure from sea level to 2,000 feet in altitude; at 12 pounds pressure from 2,001 to 4,000 feet; at 13 pounds pressure from 4,001 to 6,000 feet; at 14 pounds pressure from 6,001 to 8,000 feet.

Tomato Sauce (Hot Pack)

Quarter or chunk prepared tomatoes and simmer for 5 minutes. Press through a sieve or food mill. Simmer the tomato juice in a large diameter pot until sauce reduces and reaches the desired consistency, being careful not to scorch the bottom.

Following the instructions for water-bath canning (chapter 3) or pressure canning (chapter 4), fill prepared jars with your acidifier of choice, add salt if desired (1 tsp. per quart or ½ tsp. per pint), and fill with the hot tomato sauce, leaving ½-inch headspace.

Process for the correct amount of time as follows:

Water-Bath Canner

Jar Size	Processing time for 0 – 1,000 feet	Processing time for 1,001 – 3,000 feet	Processing time for 3,001 – 6,000 feet	Processing time above 6,000 feet
Pint	35 minutes	40 minutes	45 minutes	50 minutes
Quart	40 minutes	45 minutes	50 minutes	55 minutes

Pressure Canner

Process quarts and pints for 15 minutes as follows: Weighted gauge canner: Process at 10 pounds pressure from sea level to 1,000 feet in altitude; at 15 pounds pressure above 1,000 feet.

Dial gauge canner: Process at 11 pounds pressure from sea level to 2,000 feet in altitude; at 12 pounds pressure from 2,001 to 4,000 feet; at 13 pounds pressure from 4,001 to 6,000 feet; at 14 pounds pressure from 6,001 to 8,000 feet.

Whole Or Halved Tomatoes In Water (Hot Or Cold Pack)

Wash tomatoes and slip off skins (see "Preparing Tomatoes").

Cold pack: Fill jars with acidifier of choice, salt (if using), and peeled raw tomatoes. Cover with boiling water, leaving ½ inch headspace.

Hot pack: Put peeled tomatoes in a large pan and add enough water to cover the tomatoes. Simmer gently for 5 minutes. Fill jars with hot tomatoes and ladle the hot cooking liquid over them, leaving ½-inch headspace.

Follow the instructions for water-bath canning (chapter 3) or pressure canning (chapter 4). Process for the correct amount of time as follows: Water- Bath Canner

Jar Size	Processing time for 0 – 1,000 feet	Processing time for 1,001 – 3,000 feet	Processing time for 3,001 – 6,000 feet	Processing time above 6,000 feet
Pint	40 minutes	45 minutes	50 minutes	55 minutes
Quart	45 minutes	50 minutes	55 minutes	60 minutes

Pressure Canner

Process quarts and pints for 10 minutes as follows: Weighted gauge canner: Process at 10 pounds pressure from sea level to 1,000 feet in altitude; at 15 pounds pressure above 1,000 feet.

Dial gauge canner: Process at 11 pounds pressure from sea level to 2,000 feet in altitude; at 12 pounds pressure from 2,001 to 4,000 feet; at 13 pounds pressure from 4,001 to 6,000 feet; at 14 pounds pressure from 6,001 to 8,000 feet.

Whole Or Halved Tomatoes With No Added Liquid (Cold Pack)

Wash tomatoes and slip off skins (see "Preparing Tomatoes" above).

Fill jars with acidifier of choice and salt (if using). Pack jars with raw tomatoes, pressing on them to fill the spaces. Leave ½-inch headspace.

Follow the instructions for water-bath canning (chapter 3) or pressure canning (chapter 4).

Process for the correct amount of time as follows:

Water-Bath Canner

Jar Size	Processing time for 0 – 1,000 feet	Processing time for 1,001 – 3,000 feet	Processing time for 3,001 – 6,000 feet	Processing time above 6,000 feet
Pint	85 minutes	90 minutes	95 minutes	100 minutes
Quart	85 minutes	90 minutes	95 minutes	100 minutes

Pressure Canner

Process quarts and pints for 25 minutes as follows: Weighted gauge canner: Process at 10 pounds pressure from sea level to 1,000 feet in altitude; at 15 pounds pressure above 1,000 feet.

Dial gauge canner: Process at 11 pounds pressure from sea level to 2,000 feet in altitude; at 12 pounds pressure from 2,001 to 4,000 feet; at 13 pounds pressure from 4,001 to 6,000 feet; at 14 pounds pressure from 6,001 to 8,000 feet.

Blender Catsup

- 24 lbs. tomatoes
- 2 lbs. onions
- 1 lb. red bell peppers
- 1 lb. green bell peppers
- 9 cups 5% vinegar
- 9 cups sugar
- ½ cup salt
- 3 T. dry mustard
- 1½ T. ground red pepper
- 1½ tsp. whole allspice
- 1½ T. whole cloves
- 3 sticks cinnamon

Preparing

Combine allspice, cloves, and cinnamon in a spice bag, tie shut, and set aside for now.

Wash tomatoes and then skin them by plunging them into boiling water for 30 to 60 seconds or until skins begin to split. Dip them in cold water and then slip off the skins. Core and quarter the skinned tomatoes. Remove seeds from the peppers and slice into strips. Peel and quarter onions.

Working in batches, blend tomatoes, peppers, and onions at high speed for about 5 seconds in electric blender. Pour the sauce into a large stockpot and boil gently for an hour, stirring frequently so it doesn't scorch.

Add vinegar, sugar, salt, dry mustard, ground red pepper, and the filled spice bag. Continue boiling and stirring until the sauce is very thick and has been reduced by about half. Remove spice bag.

Fill pint jars with the hot catsup, leaving ⅛-inch headspace. Process pints in a boiling water canner for 15 minutes at 0 to 1,000 feet, 20 minutes at 1,001 to

6,000 feet, or 25 minutes at 6,001 to 8,000 feet.

Classic Tomato Catsup

- 24 lbs. tomatoes
- 3 cups onions, chopped

- ¾ tsp. ground hot red pepper (such as cayenne)
- 3 cups 5% cider vinegar
- 4 tsp. whole cloves
- 3 sticks cinnamon, broken
- 1½ tsp. whole allspice
- 3 T. celery seeds
- 1½ cups sugar
- ¼ cup salt

Preparing

Wash and skin tomatoes by dropping them into a pot of boiling water for 30 to 60 seconds or until skins begin to split. Plunge into cold water and slip off the skins. Remove cores. Quarter tomatoes and place in a large stockpot. Add onions and red pepper. Bring to a boil and then simmer uncovered for 20 minutes, stirring frequently.

Combine cloves, cinnamon, allspice, and celery seeds in a spice bag—you can make one using several layers of cheesecloth tied shut so the spices don't escape. In a small pot, add the filled spice bag along with the cider vinegar and bring to a boil. Turn off the heat and let the vinegar mixture sit on the hot burner while the tomatoes are simmering for 20 minutes.

Next, remove the spice bag from the vinegar and mix together the vinegar and tomatoes. Boil for 30 minutes, stirring frequently.

Put the tomato and vinegar mixture through a food mill or sieve and return the sauce to the large pot. Add the sugar and salt and then boil gently, stirring frequently so as not to burn the sauce. Simmer this mixture until it becomes very thick and the volume has been reduced by about half.

Fill pint jars with the hot catsup, leaving ⅛-inch headspace. Process pints in a boiling water canner for 15 minutes at 0 to 1000 feet, 20 minutes at 1,001 to

6,000 feet, or 25 minutes at 6,001 to 8,000 feet. Makes about 7 pints.

Easy Tomato Catsup

- 3 quarts tomato juice
- 1 pint 5% cider vinegar

- 4 to 5 cups sugar (to taste)
- 1 tsp. salt
- ¼ tsp. pepper
- 3 drops clove oil (optional: 4 tsp. whole cloves)
- 5 drops cinnamon oil (optional: 3 sticks cinnamon, broken into pieces)
- 4 T. dry mustard

Preparing

If using whole spices, place them into a spice bag (you can use several layers of cheesecloth with the top tied shut).

In a large pot, mix together all ingredients—if using the spice bag, add that into the pot as well. Boil gently, stirring frequently so the mixture doesn't scorch, for about 2 to 2½ hours until very thick. Remove spice bag.

Fill pint jars with the hot catsup, leaving ⅛-inch headspace. Process pints in a boiling water canner for 15 minutes at 0 to1,000 feet, 20 minutes at 1,001 to 6,000 feet, or 25 minutes at 6,001 to 8,000 feet. Makes about 4 to 5 pints.

Hot Chili Salsa

- 3 quarts tomatoes, skinned, cored, and chopped
- 2 quarts chili peppers, chopped*
- 2½ cups onions, peeled and chopped
- 1 cup vinegar (5% strength)
- 3 tsp. salt
- ½ tsp. Pepper

Preparing

Use a combination of peppers depending on the amount of heat you want: bell and Anaheim peppers are milder, while jalapeno and Serrano peppers are hotter.

Combine all ingredients in a large pot, heat to boiling, and then simmer for 10 minutes, stirring frequently so it doesn't scorch.

Fill pint jars with the hot salsa, leaving ⅛-inch headspace. Process pints in a boiling water canner for 15 minutes at 0 to 1,000 feet, 20 minutes at 1,001 to

6,000 feet, or 25 minutes at 6,001 to 8,000 feet. Makes about 7 pints.

Kropfs' Best Salsa

- 1 gallon tomatoes, peeled and diced
- 4 to 5 Serrano chili peppers, diced
- 6 to 7 cups onions, peeled and diced
- 1 cup green bell pepper, diced
- 1½ cups 5% vinegar
- 3 T. salt
- 1½ T. garlic salt
- 1½ tsp. minced garlic

Preparing

If your tomatoes have a lot of seeds, remove some of the seeds before cooking. Be careful with the Serrano peppers—they're hot! Use gloves when handling and wash your hands thoroughly when done.

Combine all ingredients in a large pot and bring to a boil; simmer uncovered, stirring frequently to prevent scorching, for about 2 hours.

Fill pint jars with the hot salsa, leaving ⅛-inch headspace. Process pints in a boiling water canner for 15 minutes at 0 to 1,000 feet, 20 minutes at 1,001 to

6,000 feet, or 25 minutes at 6,001 to 8,000 feet. Makes about 8 pints.

Spaghetti Sauce Without Meat

- 30 lbs. tomatoes (about 4½ gallons)
- 1 cup onions, peeled and chopped (don't use more!)
- 1 cup celery or bell pepper, chopped (or use a combination, but no more than 1 cup total)
- 1 lb. mushrooms, sliced (optional; don't use more!)
- 5 cloves garlic, minced
- 2 T. vegetable oil
- 2 T. salt or to taste
- 2 tsp. black pepper
- 2 T. oregano
- ¼ cup parsley, minced

- ¼ cup brown sugar

Preparing

Skin tomatoes by plunging them into boiling water for about 30 to 60 seconds or until skins start to split. Remove and dip into cold water; slip off loosened skins. Remove cores and quarter the tomatoes. Place in a large pot and boil uncovered for 20 minutes. Push through a food mill or sieve and return to the large pot.

In a smaller saucepan, sauté onions, celery or bell pepper, mushrooms, and garlic in the vegetable oil until tender.

Combine the sautéed vegetables with the sauced tomatoes in the large pot; add salt, pepper, spices, and sugar. Bring to a boil, stirring frequently so the sauce doesn't scorch. Reduce heat and simmer, uncovered, until thick and reduced by about a third. Stir frequently to prevent the bottom from scorching.

Fill jars, leaving 1-inch headspace. Process pints for 20 minutes and quarts for 25 minutes in a pressure canner as follows: Weighted gauge canner: Process at 10 pounds pressure from sea level to 1,000 feet in altitude; at 15 pounds pressure above 1,000 feet.

Dial gauge canner: Process at 11 pounds pressure from sea level to 2,000 feet in altitude; at 12 pounds pressure from 2,001 to 4,000 feet; at 13 pounds pressure from 4,001 to 6,000 feet; at 14 pounds pressure from 6,001 to 8,000 feet.

Makes about 4½ quarts or 9 pints.

Spaghetti Sauce With Meat

- 30 lb. tomatoes (about 4½ gallons)
- 2½ lbs. ground beef
- 1 cup onions, peeled and chopped (don't use more!)
- 1 cup celery or bell pepper, chopped (or use a combination, but no more than 1 cup total)
- 1 lb. mushrooms, sliced (optional; don't use more!)
- 5 cloves garlic, minced
- 2 T. salt or to taste
- 2 tsp. black pepper

- 2 T. oregano
- ¼ cup parsley, minced
- ¼ cup brown sugar

Preparing

Skin tomatoes by plunging them into boiling water for about 30 to 60 seconds or until skins start to split. Remove and dip into cold water; slip off loosened skins. Remove cores and quarter the tomatoes. Place in a large pot and boil uncovered for 20 minutes. Put through a food mill or sieve and return to the large pot.

In a smaller saucepan, brown the hamburger and drain off fat. Add onions, celery or bell pepper, mushrooms, and garlic and sauté until tender. Add to the sauced tomatoes in the large pot along with the salt, pepper, herbs, and sugar.

Bring to a boil, stirring frequently. Reduce heat and simmer uncovered, stirring frequently so the bottom doesn't scorch, until the sauce is thick and reduced by about a third.

Fill jars, leaving 1-inch headspace. Process pints for 60 minutes and quarts for 70 minutes in a pressure canner as follows: Weighted gauge canner: Process at 10 pounds pressure from sea level to 1,000 feet in altitude; at 15 pounds pressure above 1,000 feet.

Dial gauge canner: Process at 11 pounds pressure from sea level to 2,000 feet in altitude; at 12 pounds pressure from 2,001 to 4,000 feet; at 13 pounds pressure from 4,001 to 6,000 feet; at 14 pounds pressure from 6,001 to 8,000 feet.

Makes about 4½ quarts or 9 pints.

Chapter 9: Fruit & Pie Filling

Canning fruit when the summer harvest is in full swing makes good sense. You can purchase fruit at the best prices during this time because there is such an abundance when the fruits are in season. And if you grow some of your own fruit, head out to your local U-pick farm stand, or find a patch of wild berries or apples to pick, your cost will be lower still. Just make sure that if you pick "wild," you aren't inadvertently taking someone else's produce. In some areas of the country, there are abandoned or vacant homesteads and it may seem that the fruit is there for the taking, but it's likely that the land is owned by someone. So ask first before you pick. Or offer to do the picking for the owner in exchange for half of the harvest.

Fruit

When gathering or purchasing fruit for canning, pick only as much as you think you can process within a short period of time so the fruit remains in good condition. The fruit should be ripe, and any spots on the fruit that are bruised or blemished should be cut out before processing. When you are preparing the fruit work quickly in one session; never let the fruit sit for long periods during this time.

Canning Fruit With Sugar Syrup

It's possible to safely can fruit without using sweet syrup. You can use juice or water instead. But you will have to hot pack unsweetened fruit (by first boiling the fruit before placing in the hot jars), and the sugar syrup tends to plump up the fruit and keep them slightly firmer during the canning process. For years I canned my fruit using water, but I've since gone to using a lightly sweetened syrup instead, and I think my canned fruit is better for that change. But suit yourself.

Here is a handy guide for making different strengths of syrup for your fruit canning needs:

Syrup Strength	Amount of Sugar	Amount of Water	Yield
Extra-light	1¼ cups	5½ cups	6 cups
Light	2¼ cups	5¼ cups	6½ cups
Medium	3¼ cups	5 cups	7 cups
Heavy	4¼ cups	4¼ cups	7 cups

Mix together the sugar and water and heat gently, stirring, until the sugar is completely dissolved. If you don't use the entire batch of syrup in a canning session, you can always refrigerate it and use for the next batch.

Total Fruit Required Per Quart Jar

Fruit Variety	Pounds per Quart Jar
Apples	2¾
Applesauce	3
Apricots	2¼
Asian Pears	2½
Berries	1¾
Cherries	2½
Figs	2½
Grapefruit	2
Grapes	2
Nectarines	2½
Oranges	2
Peaches	2½
Pears	2½
Pineapple	3
Plums	2
Rhubarb	1½

Preparing & Processing The Fruit

Light-colored fruits such as apples, apricots, nectarines, peaches, and pears should be held in an anti-darkening, acidified water solution so they don't darken. You can use 1 tsp. of ascorbic acid or citric acid dissolved into each gallon of water used or ¾ cup of lemon juice stirred in per gallon.

When canning, follow the directions in "Water-Bath Canning Guide" in chapter 3.

Apples

Wash, peel, core, and slice the apples. Place the prepared fruit in the anti- darkening solution (above). When all of the apples have been sliced, drain and rinse the apples before putting them into a large pot. Boil apple slices 5 minutes in a sugar syrup solution of your choice (see "Sugar Syrup for Canning Fruit" for syrup recipe) or water. Pack hot fruit into hot jars, leaving ½-inch headspace; cover with the boiling cooking liquid and process in a water-bath canner for the correct amount of time as follows:

Jar Size	Processing time for 0 – 1,000 feet	Processing time for 1,001 – 3,000 feet	Processing time for 3,001 – 6,000 feet	Processing time above 6,000 feet
Pint	20 minutes	25 minutes	30 minutes	35 minutes
Quart	20 minutes	25 minutes	30 minutes	35 minutes

Applesauce

Wash and chunk the apples. Remove seeds. (There's no need to peel them.) Simmer, stirring frequently, until soft. You may add a small amount of water to prevent the apples from sticking if necessary. Put the apples through a food mill or sieve. Add sugar to taste if desired. Reheat the applesauce to simmering. Pack hot fruit into hot jars, leaving ½ inch headspace; and process in a water-bath canner for the correct amount of time as follows:

Jar Size	Processing time for 0 – 1,000 feet	Processing time for 1,001 – 3,000 feet	Processing time for 3,001 – 6,000 feet	Processing time above 6,000 feet
Pint	15 minutes	20 minutes	25 minutes	30 minutes
Quart	20 minutes	25 minutes	30 minutes	35 minutes

Apricots

Wash and halve the fruit (no need to peel). Remove pits. Use an anti-darkening solution to prevent the apricots from turning brown. Drain, rinse, and drain again.

To hot pack apricots, heat the fruit in sugar syrup or water until heated through and then pack hot into hot jars, leaving ½-inch headspace.

To raw pack apricots, pack the raw, unheated fruit into the jars and poor boiling water or syrup over them, leaving ½ inch headspace.

Process in a water-bath canner for the correct amount of time as follows:

Jar Size	Processing time for 0 – 1,000 feet	Processing time for 1,001 – 3,000 feet	Processing time for 3,001 – 6,000 feet	Processing time above 6,000 feet
Pint	Hot pack: 20 minutes Raw pack: 25 minutes	Hot pack: 25 minutes Raw pack: 30 minutes	Hot pack: 30 minutes Raw pack: 35 minutes	Hot pack: 35 minutes Raw pack: 40 minutes
Quart	Hot pack: 25 minutes Raw pack: 30 minutes	Hot pack: 30 minutes Raw pack: 35 minutes	Hot pack: 35 minutes Raw pack: 40 minutes	Hot pack: 40 minutes Raw pack: 45 minutes

Berries (Blackberries, Blueberries, Raspberries)

Note: Strawberries do not can well.

To hot pack, bring berries and ½ cup sugar per quart of berries to a boil in covered pot. Shake pot frequently to prevent scorching and sticking.

To raw pack, tightly pack berries into jars. Cover with boiling syrup and process in a water-bath canner for the correct amount of time as follows:

Jar Size	Processing time for 0 – 1,000 feet	Processing time for 1,001 – 3,000 feet	Processing time for 3,001 – 6,000 feet	Processing time above 6,000 feet
Pint	Hot pack: 15 minutes Raw pack: 15 minutes	Hot pack: 20 minutes Raw pack: 20 minutes	Hot pack: 20 minutes Raw pack: 20 minutes	Hot pack: 25 minutes Raw pack: 25 minutes
Quart	Hot pack: 15 minutes Raw pack: 20 minutes	Hot pack: 20 minutes Raw pack: 25 minutes	Hot pack: 25 minutes Raw pack: 30 minutes	Hot pack: 30 minutes Raw pack: 35 minutes

Cherries

Wash cherries and remove pits if desired; it's not necessary to remove the pits before canning.

To hot pack cherries, heat cherries and syrup or water in a large pot until boiling. Pack hot cherries in hot jars and cover with hot cooking liquid, leaving ½-inch headspace.

To raw pack cherries, heat syrup or water (if canning sour cherries, it's best to use a medium or heavy syrup); keep syrup hot. Ladle some hot syrup into hot jars (¼ cup for pints; ½ cup for quarts). Fill jars with cherries, taking care to tightly pack cherries without crushing them. Leave ½-inch headspace. Add more syrup if necessary to cover cherries, maintaining ½-inch headspace.

Process the cherries in a water-bath canner for the correct amount of time as follows:

Jar Size	Processing time for 0 – 1,000 feet	Processing time for 1,001 – 3,000 feet	Processing time for 3,001 – 6,000 feet	Processing time above 6,000 feet
Pint	Hot pack: 15 minutes Raw pack: 25 minutes	Hot pack: 20 minutes Raw pack: 30 minutes	Hot pack: 20 minutes Raw pack: 35 minutes	Hot pack: 25 minutes Raw pack: 40 minutes
Quart	Hot pack: 20 minutes Raw pack: 25 minutes	Hot pack: 25 minutes Raw pack: 30 minutes	Hot pack: 30 minutes Raw pack: 35 minutes	Hot pack: 35 minutes Raw pack: 40 minutes

Citrus (Grapefruit, Mandarins, Oranges, Tangerines, etc.)

Wash and peel. Remove as much of the white membrane as possible, as this will turn bitter when canned if left on. Remove seeds. Pull apart the sections.

Pack pint jars with citrus fruit sections, pour boiling syrup over the fruit to cover, leaving ½-inch headspace. Do not use quart jars.

Process pints in a boiling water canner for 10 minutes at 0 to 1,000 feet, 15 minutes at 1,001 to 6,000 feet, or 20 minutes at 6,001 to 8,000 feet.

Figs

Select firm, ripe figs; do not choose fruit that has very soft flesh. Do not peel or remove stems. Figs must be hot packed; do not raw pack.

To hot pack figs, put the fruit in a large pot, cover with water, and boil 2 minutes. Drain. Place the figs back into the large pot, add light syrup, and boil gently for 5 minutes.

Figs need additional acid in order to be safely processed. Before adding the figs, add 2 tablespoons bottled lemon juice per quart jar or 1 tablespoon bottled lemon juice per pint jar. Fill the jars with figs and cover with cooking liquid.

Process in water-bath canner for the correct amount of time as follows:

Jar Size	Processing time for 0 – 1,000 feet	Processing time for 1,001 – 3,000 feet	Processing time for 3,001 – 6,000 feet	Processing time above 6,000 feet
Pint	45 minutes	50 minutes	55 minutes	60 minutes
Quart	50 minutes	55 minutes	60 minutes	65 minutes

Fruit Juice (Apple, Berry, Citrus, Grape, or Pineapple)

Wash fruit. Remove pits or seeds. Crush fruit. Heat fruit to simmering, stirring frequently to prevent sticking and scorching. When fruit is very soft, strain juice through a bag or use several layers of dampened cheesecloth. When the juice has completely drained, measure juice and add about 1 cup sugar per gallon, or to taste.

Reheat juice to simmering and then pour hot juice into jars, leaving ¼-inch headspace. Process in water-bath canner for the correct amount of time as follows;

Jar Size	Processing time for 0 – 1,000 feet	Processing time for 1,001 – 3,000 feet	Processing time for 3,001 – 6,000 feet	Processing time above 6,000 feet
Pint	5 minutes	10 minutes	10 minutes	15 minutes
Quart	5 minutes	10 minutes	10 minutes	15 minutes

Nectarines

Nectarines do not need to be peeled. Halve, quarter, or slice the nectarines, removing the pit. Use an acid water solution to prevent darkening when working with them. Follow the directions and processing times for apricots.

Peaches

To peel the skins of peaches, plunge clean peaches into boiling water for 45–60 seconds or until skins just begin to crack. Rinse peaches in cold water and then slip off the skins; remove pit. Halve, quarter, or slice the peaches. Use an acid water solution to prevent darkening when working with them. Follow the directions and processing times for apricots.

Pears (plus Asian Pears*)

Carefully peel pears. Halve, quarter, or slice them. Remove the core and seeds. Use an acid water solution to prevent darkening when working with them. Follow the directions and processing times for apricots.

If canning Asian pears, you must add lemon juice. Add 2 tablespoons bottled lemon juice per quart jar or 1 tablespoon bottled lemon juice per pint jar.

Plums

Plums may be canned whole or halved. Remove stems and wash. If canning whole, prick two sides of the plum with a fork to break the skin and prevent the fruit from splitting. The pit doesn't get removed. If halved, go ahead and remove the pit.

To hot pack, add plums to hot syrup and boil 2 minutes. Cover the pot and let set for 20 to 30 minutes. Fill jars with hot plums and cover them with the hot cooking liquid. Leave ½-inch headspace.

To raw pack, fill jars with raw plums, packing firmly. Cover with boiling syrup, leaving ½ inch headspace.

Process in a water-bath canner as follows: Hot pack: 20 minutes for pints and 25 minutes for quarts Raw pack: 25 minutes for pints and 30 minutes for quarts

Rhubarb

Wash rhubarb and cut into ½-inch pieces. Measure the amount of rhubarb you have and then place it in a pot. Add ½ cup sugar for each quart of fruit and mix gently but thoroughly. Let mixture set to draw out the juice, about 30 minutes. Bring the rhubarb and syrup to a boil.

Fill pint jars with the hot rhubarb and syrup, leaving ½-inch headspace. Process pints in a boiling water canner for 15 minutes at 0 to 1,000 feet, 20 minutes at 1,001 to 6,000 feet, or 25 minutes over 6,000 feet.

Pie Filling

Having canned pie filling on your pantry shelves means you can throw together a sweet treat quickly and easily anytime the mood strikes or unexpected guests arrive on your doorstep. In fact, you don't even need to use these pie fillings to make pies—they are equally good spooned over ice cream, French toast, or chiffon cake, added to coffee cakes or muffins, or used to make fruit crisps and cobblers.

You can use a bit less or more of the sugar and spices listed in each of the pie filling recipes to suit your tastes, but always use the amount of lemon juice called for in the recipe. This will ensure that your canned pie filling is safe once it's canned.

When working with light-colored fruits such as apples and peaches, place the cut slices in an anti-darkening, acidified water solution so they don't turn brown after they are cut. You can use 1 tsp. of ascorbic acid or citric acid dissolved into each gallon of water used or ¾ cup of lemon juice stirred in per gallon. When all your fruit has been prepared, drain it, give it a quick rinse, and drain again.

And remember: When canning your pie fillings, follow the directions for water-bath canning in chapter 3.

About Clear-Jel

All of the pie filling recipes in this chapter call for Clear-Jel. This is a type of cornstarch that has been made in such a way that it won't separate or become runny once canned. If you can't obtain Clear-Jel where you live, try buying a supply online, or substitute cornstarch. If your pie filling separates or becomes runny, you can always add some tapioca granules to the filling when you get ready to bake your pie to help thicken the filling, but it's not necessary. Your pie will taste just as good…but you might have to eat it with a spoon. If that happens, just tell your family you made a double crust cobbler—they'll be pleased either way!

Single Fruit Pie Filling Recipes

Use fresh fruit for each of these recipes. While it is possible to make canned pie filling using frozen fruit, the end results won't be as pleasing, so use freshly picked ripe fruit whenever you can.

The recipes that follow each make 7 quarts of pie filling, enough for one canner load in most canners. Each quart will make one 8-inch pie.

Apple Pie Filling

- 6 quarts tart pie-type apples (such as Granny Smith, Gravenstein, Jonagold, Jonathan, and Pippin)
- 5½ cups sugar
- 1½ cups Clear-Jel or cornstarch
- 1 T. cinnamon
- 1 tsp. nutmeg (optional)
- 2½ cups cold water (or use apple juice for more flavor)
- 5 cups apple juice
- ¾ cup bottled lemon juice

Preparing

Wash, peel, core and slice apples ½-inch thick. Keep them in an anti-darkening, acidified water solution so they don't darken while you are preparing the fruit. You can use 1 tsp. of ascorbic or citric acid dissolved into each gallon of water used or ¾ cup of lemon juice stirred in per gallon. Blanch the sliced apples in batches by placing them in a gallon of boiling water for 1 minute. Remove apples, drain, and place them in a covered pot to keep warm.

Combine sugar, Clear-Jel, and spices in another large pot. Add the water and/or apple juice and cook over medium high heat, stirring constantly, until mixture thickens and begins to bubble. To the pot of cooking liquid, add the lemon juice and boil for 1 minute, stirring constantly. Fold in the apples.

Fill quart jars, leaving 1-inch headspace. Following the directions in "Water- Bath Canning Guide," process the filling in pint or quart jars in a boiling water canner for 25 minutes at 0 to 1,000 feet, 30 minutes at 1,001 to 3,000 feet, or 35 minutes at 3,001 feet and over.

To Use: Open a jar of apple pie filling and spoon into a baked or unbaked 8-inch pie shell. Cover with a top crust if desired and bake in a preheated 425° oven for 20 to 25 minutes, or until the crust is baked and golden and the filling is hot.

Blackberry Pie Filling

- 6 quarts blackberries, stems and caps removed
- 7 cups sugar
- 1¾ cups Clear-Jel or cornstarch
- 9⅓ cups cold water (you can substitute berry juice for some or all of the water for a richer fruit flavor)
- ½ cup bottled lemon juice

Preparing

Wash blackberries by very gently rinsing and draining them.

In a large pot, combine sugar and Clear-Jel and stir to mix. Add the water and/or juice and cook over medium high heat, stirring constantly, until mixture thickens and begins to bubble. Add the lemon juice and boil 1 minute, continuing to stir constantly. Gently stir in blackberries.

Fill quart jars, leaving 1-inch headspace. Following the directions in "Water- Bath Canning Guide," process the filling in pint or quart jars in a boiling water canner for 30 minutes at 0 to 1,000 feet, 35 minutes at 1,001 to 3,000 feet, or 40 minutes at 3,001 feet and over.

To Use: Open a jar of blackberry pie filling and spoon into a baked or unbaked 8-inch pie shell. Cover with a top crust if desired and bake in a preheated 425° oven for 20 to 25 minutes, or until the crust is baked and golden and the filling is hot.

Blueberry Pie Filling

- 6 quarts blueberries
- 6 cups sugar
- 2¼ cups Clear-Jel or cornstarch

- 7 cups cold water or juice (you can substitute berry or grape juice for some or all of the water)
- ½ cup bottled lemon juice

Preparing

Remove blossom bits and stems. Carefully wash and drain the blueberries.

In a large pot, mix together the Clear-Jel and sugar. Add the water and/or juice and cook over medium high heat, stirring constantly, until mixture thickens and begins to bubble. Add the lemon juice and continue to boil, stirring constantly, for 1 minute. Stir in blueberries and cook until heated through.

Fill quart jars, leaving 1½-inch headspace. Following the directions in "Water- Bath Canning Guide," process the filling in pint or quart jars in a boiling water canner for 30 minutes at 0 to 1,000 feet, 35 minutes at 1,001 to 3,000 feet, or 40 minutes at 3,001 feet and over.

To Use: Open a jar of blueberry pie filling and spoon into a baked or unbaked 8- inch pie shell.

Cover with a top crust if desired and bake in a preheated 425° oven for 20 to 25 minutes, or until the crust is baked and golden and the filling is hot.

Cherry Pie Filling

- 6 quarts sour (pie) cherries
- 7 cups sugar
- 1¾ cup Clear-Jel or cornstarch
- 9⅓ cups cold water or juice (you can substitute cherry juice for some or all of the water)
- ½ cup bottled lemon juice

Preparing

Rinse and pit cherries. Keep them in an anti-darkening, acidified water solution so they don't darken while you are preparing the fruit. You can use 1 tsp. of ascorbic or citric acid dissolved into each gallon of water used, or ¾ cup of lemon juice stirred in per gallon.

In a large pot, combine sugar and Clear-Jel and stir to mix. Add the water and/or juice and cook over medium high heat, stirring constantly, until mixture thickens and begins to bubble. Add the lemon juice and boil 1 minute, continuing to stir constantly. Gently stir in cherries.

Fill quart jars, leaving 1-inch headspace. Following the directions in "Water- Bath Canning Guide," process the filling in pint or quart jars in a boiling water canner for 25 minutes at 0 to 1,000 feet, 30 minutes at 1,001 to 3,000 feet, or 35 minutes at 3,001 feet and over.

To Use: Open a jar of cherry pie filling and spoon into a baked or unbaked 8- inch pie shell. Cover with a top crust if desired and bake in a preheated 425° oven for 20 to 25 minutes, or until the crust is baked and golden and the filling is hot.

Peach Pie Filling

- 6 quarts sliced peaches
- 7 cups sugar
- 2 cups + 3 T. Clear-Jel or cornstarch
- 5¼ cups cold water
- 1¾ cups bottled lemon juice

Preparing

Peel peaches: To loosen skins so they slip off, plunge peaches into boiling water for 45 to 60 seconds and then rinse them in cold water. The skins will have begun to crack and peel and should come off easily. Slice the peaches and keep them in an anti-darkening, acidified water solution so they don't darken while you are preparing the fruit. You can use 1 tsp. of ascorbic or citric acid dissolved into each gallon of water used or ¾ cup of lemon juice stirred in per gallon. In a large pot, combine sugar and Clear-Jel and stir to mix. Add the cold water and cook over medium high heat, stirring constantly, until mixture thickens and begins to bubble. Add the lemon juice and boil 1 minute, continuing to stir constantly. Gently stir in peach slices and continue to cook for 3 more minutes.

Fill quart jars, leaving 1-inch headspace. Following the directions in "Water- Bath Canning Guide," process the filling in pint or quart jars in a boiling water canner for 30 minutes at 0 to 1,000 feet, 35 minutes at 1,001 to 3,000 feet, or 40 minutes at 3,001 feet and over.

To Use: Open a jar of peach pie filling and spoon into a baked or unbaked 8-inch pie shell. Cover with a top crust if desired and bake in a preheated 425° oven for 20–25 minutes, or until the crust is baked and golden and the filling is hot.

With all that stated, to check out my other books on amazon, visit my Authors page, Emily Fisher Books

Chapter 10: Vegetables

When you add canned vegetables to your stash of pantry items, you will have much more to choose from when preparing well-balanced meals for yourself and your loved ones during the cold winter months. Because they are a low-acid food, you must use a pressure canner to safely can vegetables. Follow the directions and don't deviate and you can rest assured that your jars of food are safe to eat.

When you pick or purchase vegetables to process by canning, it's best to gather only as much as you are able to process in a day. Vegetables that sit for too long before being canned can become overripe and begin to mold and decay. This will compromise the quality of your food and also heighten the possibility that the food will spoil in the jar. And of course you'll want to avoid choosing any vegetable that shows signs of decay. If there are some blemishes, you can trim those areas away as long as the part of the vegetable you do use is in good shape.

How To Inspect Jars for Food Spoilage

When you plan to use some of your home-canned low-acid vegetables, it's a good idea to inspect the jar and contents before using. Obviously, if the jar has an unsealed lid, this is a sure sign that spoilage has occurred and you will want to dispose of the contents immediately. But even if the seal is not broken, there are other clues that the food might not be safe: If the jar lid doesn't have a tight concave center indicating a good seal, or if the lid is bulging, the food has likely spoiled.

But even when all looks good from the outside, take a moment when opening the jar to continue your inspection: Smell for unnatural odors and look for spurting liquid when you pop off the lid. Check the underside of the lid and the top surface of the food in the jar to see if there is cotton-like mold growth. (Mold can be white, blue, black, or green.) If you're using well water, the lids may look darkened due to the minerals in the water. Acidic foods in particular can cause the underside of jar lids to darken. This is perfectly fine and is not the same as toxic mold growth—the food is safe to eat.

If you suspect a jar of food has gone bad, do not taste it! Instead, dispose of the food in such a way that no people or animals can get to it. I've had food spoil a total of two times in more than 40 years of canning experience, so this really is rare. If you suspect a jar of food has gone bad, remove the lid and then place the jar with the food still in it and the loose lid upright in a pot with water to completely cover the jar. Boil for 30 minutes. Cool and dispose of the food in the garbage or by deeply burying the food in an out-of-the-way area. You can wash and sterilize the jar for reuse. Don't forget to thoroughly wash and disinfect your work area, tools used, and hands when you are done.

Total Number of Vegetables Needed per Quart Jar

Vegetable	Pounds per Quart Jar
Asparagus	3½
Beans, dried	¾ (2 cups dried beans = 1 lb. = 4 to 5 cups cooked)
Beans, green or wax	2
Beans, fresh lima or butter	4
Beets (without tops)	4
Carrots (without tops)	2½
Corn, sweet (weigh before husking)	4½ (measure weight before husking)
Corn, cream style	2¼ per pint (measure weight before husking)
Greens (spinach, chard, etc.)	4
Mushrooms	2 per pint (canned in half-pint or pint jars only)
Okra	2
Peas, fresh green or English	4½
Peppers, hot, sweet, or Bell	1 per pint
Potatoes, sweet	2½
Potatoes, white	5
Pumpkin (seeded and cubed)	2½
Winter squash	2½

Vegetables that do not can well include artichokes, avocados, bananas (mashed), broccoli,

Brussels sprouts, cabbage (pickled is fine), cauliflower (pickled is fine), eggplant, lettuce, and summer squash (such as zucchini).

How To Prepare And Process The Vegetables

In this section you will find listed the most common vegetables suitable for canning and the specific guidelines for each.

Altitude Adjustment Directions

Depending on the altitude where you are canning, you may need to adjust the psi of your canner in order to ensure that your food has been safely processed at the required high temperatures. The following chart lists the adjustments you need to make depending on where you live: Weighted gauge canner: Process at 10 pounds pressure from sea level to 1,000 feet in altitude; at 15 pounds pressure above 1,000 feet.

Dial gauge canner: Process at 11 pounds pressure from sea level to 2,000 feet in altitude; at 12 pounds pressure from 2,001 to 4,000 feet; at 13 pounds pressure from 4,001 to 6,000 feet; at 14 pounds pressure from 6,001 to 8,000 feet.

Asparagus

Wash and trim off the woody ends and remove the scales from the stalks. Rinse again. Leave whole or cut into 1-inch pieces.

Hot Pack: Cover asparagus with boiling water and boil for 2 to 3 minutes. Loosely pack hot asparagus into jars. Add salt, if desired (1 tsp. per quart, ½ tsp. per pint). Cover with cooking liquid or fresh boiling water. Leave 1-inch headspace. Following the pressure canning directions in chapter 4, process pints for 30 minutes and quarts for 40 minutes at 10 psi, adjusting the psi as necessary for your altitude according to the altitude adjustment directions above.

Raw Pack: Pack tightly in jars without crushing. Add salt, if desired (1 tsp. per quart, ½ tsp. per pint). Cover with boiling water. Following the pressure canning directions in chapter 4, process pints for 30 minutes and quarts for 40 minutes at

10 psi, adjusting the psi as necessary for altitude according to the altitude adjustment directions above.

Beans & Peas, Dried

Dried beans include varieties such as pinto, black or black turtle, kidney, red, pink, Great Northern, small white, navy, dried Lima, cranberry, and so forth. Beans are highly nutritious and inexpensive and make a great addition to your meal planning. The downside to using dried beans, however, is that they take several hours to cook—not the kind of time many of us have with our busy schedules. Store-bought canned beans could be an answer, but instead, why not can your own supply? It's so much cheaper—and easy too.

Place beans or peas in large pot and add water to cover by 2 inches. Bring to a boil and boil 2 minutes. Remove from heat, cover the pot, and let set for 1 hour. Drain. Again, add water to the beans or peas to cover by 2 inches. Bring to a boil and boil 30 minutes, stirring often.

Hot Pack Only: Pack hot beans or peas into jars. Add salt, if desired (1 tsp. per quart, ½ tsp. per pint). Cover with hot cooking liquid or boiling water, leaving 1- inch headspace. Following the pressure canning directions in chapter 4, process pints for 75 minutes and quarts for 90 minutes at 10 psi, adjusting the psi as necessary for your altitude according to the altitude adjustment directions.

Beans, Green / Wax

Wash, trim ends, and cut or snap into 1-inch pieces.

Hot Pack: Cover beans with water; bring to a boil and boil for 5 minutes. Pack beans loosely. Add salt, if desired (1 tsp. per quart, ½ tsp. per pint). Cover with boiling cooking liquid or boiling water, leaving 1-inch headspace. Following the pressure canning directions in chapter 4, process pints for 20 minutes and quarts for 25 minutes at 10 psi, adjusting the psi as necessary for your altitude according to the altitude adjustment directions.

Raw Pack: Pack beans tightly in jar. Add salt, if desired (1 tsp. per quart, ½ tsp. per pint). Cover with boiling water. Following the pressure canning directions in chapter 4, process pints for 20 minutes and quarts for 25 minutes at 10 psi, adjusting the psi as necessary for your altitude according to the altitude adjustment directions.

Beans, Fresh Lima / Butter

Shell and wash the beans.

Hot Pack: Place beans in a large pot and cover with water. Bring to a boil. Loosely pack jars, leaving 1-inch headspace. Add salt, if desired (1 tsp. per quart, ½ tsp. per pint). Cover with boiling cooking liquid or boiling water. Following the pressure canning directions in chapter 4, process pints for 40 minutes and quarts for 50 minutes at 10 psi, adjusting the psi as necessary for your altitude according to the altitude adjustment directions.

Raw Pack: Loosely pack beans into jars. For small beans, leave 1-inch headspace in pint jars and

1½-inch in quarts. For large beans, leave ¾-inch headspace in pint jars and 1¼-inch in quarts. Add salt, if desired (1 tsp. per quart, ½ tsp. per pint). Cover with boiling cooking liquid or boiling water. Following the pressure canning directions in chapter 4, process pints for 40 minutes and quarts for 50 minutes at 10 psi, adjusting the psi as necessary for your altitude according to the altitude adjustment directions.

Beets

Cut off tops of beets, leaving 1 inch of the stem and root. Wash beets, put them in a large pot, and cover with water. Bring to a boil and boil 15 to 25 minutes or until the skins slip off. Drain and set aside until cool enough to handle. Slip the skins off and trim the stem and root ends. You can leave small beets whole; cut or slice medium or large beets into ½-inch cubes or slices. Halve or quarter very large slices. Pack jars. Add salt, if desired (1 tsp. per quart, ½ tsp. per pint). Cover beets with boiling water, leaving 1-inch headspace. Following the pressure canning directions in chapter 4, process pints for 30 minutes and quarts for 35 minutes at 10 psi, adjusting the psi as necessary for your altitude according to the altitude adjustment directions.

Carrots

Wash, peel, and slice carrots.

Hot Pack: In a large pot, cover carrots with water and bring to a boil. Pack into jars. Add salt, if desired (1 tsp. per quart, ½ tsp. per pint). Cover with the boiling cooking liquid or boiling water, leaving 1-inch headspace. Following the pressure canning directions in chapter 4, process pints for 25 minutes and quarts for 30 minutes at 10 psi, adjusting the psi as necessary for your altitude according to the altitude adjustment directions.

Raw Pack: Pack sliced carrots tightly into jars. Add salt, if desired (1 tsp. per quart, ½ tsp. per pint). Ladle boiling water over the carrots, leaving 1 inch headspace. Following the pressure canning directions in chapter 4, process pints for 25 minutes and quarts for 30 minutes at 10 psi, adjusting the psi as necessary for your altitude according to the altitude adjustment directions.

Corn

Note: Super sweet corn varieties are not good for canning because the kernels turn brown in the jar.

Remove corn husks and silk and then wash the ears. Cut the corn from the cob at about two-thirds kernel depth. Do not scrape cob.

Hot Pack: Measure corn and place it in a large pot, adding water to cover. Heat to boiling. Ladle hot corn and boiling cooking liquid into jars, leaving 1-inch headspace. Add salt, if desired (1 tsp. per quart, ½ tsp. per pint). Following the pressure canning directions in chapter 4, process pints for 55 minutes and quarts for 85 minutes at 10 psi, adjusting the psi as necessary for your altitude according to the altitude adjustment directions.

Raw Pack: Pack corn loosely, without shaking or pressing down. Add salt, if desired (1 tsp. per quart, ½ tsp. per pint). Ladle boiling water over corn, leaving 1-inch headspace. Following the pressure canning directions in chapter 4, process pints for 55 minutes and quarts for 85 minutes at 10 psi, adjusting the psi as necessary for your altitude according to the altitude adjustment directions.

Creamed Corn

Hot Pack Only: Remove corn husks and silk and then wash ears. Blanch ears in boiling water for 4 minutes. When cool enough to handle, cut the corn from the cob at half-kernel depth. Using a butter knife, scrape remaining corn from the cob. Measure amount of corn and "milk" and then place in a large pot. For each quart of corn, add 1 pint water. Heat to boiling. Pack in pint jars only—do not use quarts. Add salt, if desired (½ tsp. per pint). Following the pressure canning directions in chapter 4, process pints for 85 minutes at 10 psi, adjusting the psi as necessary for your altitude according to the altitude adjustment directions.

Greens—Beet, Chard, Kale, Mustard, Spinach, etc.

Wash greens thoroughly, using several changes of water. Cut away large, tough stems and midribs. Working with about a pound at a time, blanch greens by steaming for 3 to 5 minutes or until well wilted. Use a blancher basket or a cheesecloth bag to keep the greens from being submerged in the water while blanching. Loosely pack in jar, leaving 1-inch headspace. Add salt, if desired (½ tsp. per quart, ¼ tsp. per pint). Following the pressure canning directions in chapter 4, process pints for 70 minutes and quarts for 90 minutes at 10 psi, adjusting the psi as necessary for your altitude according to the altitude adjustment directions.

Mushrooms

Hot Pack Only: Trim stems. Soak in cold water for 10 minutes to remove clinging soil and then wash in clear water. Leave small mushrooms whole; cut large mushrooms into halves or slices. Place mushrooms in a pot and add water to cover. Bring to a boil and boil 5 minutes. Pack hot mushrooms into hot jars, leaving 1-inch headspace. Use half-pint or pint jars only—do not use quart jars. Add salt, if desired (½ tsp. per pint, ¼ tsp. per half-pint). Ladle boiling water over mushrooms. Following the pressure canning directions in chapter 4, process half-pints and pints for 45 minutes at 10 psi, adjusting the psi as necessary for your altitude according to the altitude adjustment directions.

Okra

Wash and drain okra. Remove stem and blossom ends. Leave whole or slice. Place okra in a large pot and add water to cover. Bring to a boil and boil for 2 minutes. Pack hot okra into hot jars, leaving 1-inch headspace. Add salt, if desired (½ tsp. per pint, 1 tsp. per quart). Following the pressure canning directions in chapter 4, process pints for 25 minutes and quarts for 40 minutes at 10 psi, adjusting the psi as necessary for your altitude according to the altitude adjustment directions.

Peas, Green

Note: Snow, sugar snap, and pod peas are not suitable for canning due to poor quality results.
Shell and wash peas.

Hot Pack: Place peas in a large pot and add water to cover. Bring to a boil and boil for 2 minutes. Pack peas loosely into jars, leaving 1-inch headspace. Add salt, if desired (1 tsp. per quart, ½ tsp. per pint). Cover peas with boiling cooking liquid or boiling water. Following the pressure canning directions in chapter 4, process pints and quarts for 40 minutes at 10 psi, adjusting the psi as necessary for your altitude according to the altitude adjustment directions.

Raw Pack: Pack peas into jars without pressing or shaking down. Add salt, if desired (1 tsp. per quart, ½ tsp. per pint). Cover with boiling water. Following the pressure canning directions in chapter 4, process pints and quarts for 40 minutes at 10 psi, adjusting the psi as necessary for your altitude according to the altitude adjustment directions

Peppers, Hot (Jalapeno, Anaheim, Serrano, Etc.)

Wearing disposable rubber gloves, wash peppers, remove cores and seeds. Remove skins (see below). Using only half-pint or pint jars (do not use quarts!), pack peppers loosely, leaving 1-inch headspace. Add salt, if desired (½ tsp. per pint, ¼ tsp. per half-pint). Following the pressure canning directions in chapter 4, process half-pints and pints for 35 minutes at 10 psi, adjusting the psi as necessary for your altitude according to the altitude adjustment directions.

To remove skins: Blister the skins in a very hot oven (400° to a broil) or over an open flame such as an outdoor barbeque or gas grill. Turn the peppers often to blister evenly and prevent scorching. Cool peppers before removing the skin. When working with hot peppers, wear rubber gloves and keep hands away from your face, especially your eyes.

Peppers, Sweet

Note: You must use vinegar to safely process sweet peppers. Use half-pint and pint jars only—
do not use quarts.

Wash peppers and remove stems, seeds, and white ribs. Cut peppers into quarters. Place peppers in a large pot and add water to cover. Bring to a boil and boil for 3 minutes. Pack hot peppers into hot jars, leaving 1-inch headspace.

Half-Pints: Add ¼ tsp. salt and ½ T. vinegar to each jar.

Pints: Add ½ tsp. salt and 1 T. vinegar to each jar.

Following the pressure canning directions in chapter 4, process half-pints and pints for 35 minutes at 10 psi, adjusting the psi as necessary for your altitude according to the altitude adjustment directions.

Potatoes, Sweet

Wash potatoes to remove clinging soil. Boil sweet potatoes just until peel can be easily slipped off; peel potatoes and cut into quarters or cubes. Pack hot potatoes into hot jars, leaving 1-inch headspace. Ladle boiling water or a light to medium sugar syrup over sweet potatoes. Following the pressure canning directions in chapter 4, process pints for 65 minutes and quarts for 90 minutes at 10 psi, adjusting the psi as necessary for your altitude according to the altitude adjustment directions.

Potatoes, White

Wash and peel potatoes.

Cubed Potatoes: Cut potatoes into ½-inch cubes. To prevent potatoes from darkening, keep them in a brine of 1 tsp. salt per quart of water. When ready to place in jars, rinse and drain. Place in a large pot and add water to cover. Bring to a boil and boil for 2 minutes.

Whole Potatoes: You can keep small to medium potatoes whole if you prefer. Boil the whole peeled potatoes for 10 minutes and drain.

Pack hot potatoes into hot jars and ladle fresh boiling water into jars, leaving 1- inch headspace. Add salt, if desired (1 tsp. per quart, ½ tsp. per pint). Following the pressure canning directions in chapter 4, process pints for 35 minutes and quarts for 40 minutes at 10 psi, adjusting the psi as necessary for your altitude according to the altitude adjustment directions.

Pumpkin & Other Winter Squash, Cubed

Note: It is not considered safe to home-can mashed or pureed pumpkin or winter squash, but cubed is fine. If you want to use your canned pumpkin for pies, simply mash the canned pumpkin when ready to bake.

Wash pumpkin or squash. Remove seeds and scrape off fibrous strings. Peel and cut into 1-inch cubes. Place cubes of pumpkin or squash into a large pot and add just enough water to cover. Bring to a boil and boil for 2 minutes. Pack hot pumpkin into hot jars, leaving 1-inch headspace. Add salt, if desired (1 tsp. per quart, ½ tsp. per pint). Following the pressure canning directions in chapter 4, process pints for 55 minutes and quarts for 90 minutes at 10 psi, adjusting the psi as necessary for your altitude according to the altitude adjustment directions.

Alright guys with all that stated, if you're getting value from this book don't forget to leave your honest review, thanks a lot.

Chapter 11: Meat, Poultry, & Fish

When you choose to include canned meat on your food shelves, your possibilities for varied and delicious meals are enhanced and increased. Also, if there are hunters or fishermen in your family, canning is a logical way to preserve all that fresh meat. And if you are among the many folks who choose to produce some of your own meat, the possibilities widen further still.

Or maybe there's a great sale on at your local grocery store and you want to take advantage of the low price—buy plenty and can it up. Another plus is that if dinnertime is looming and you realize you have nothing thawed, a quick trip to the pantry will yield the makings of dinner in a hurry. Canning meat just makes good sense.

Tips For Canning Meat, Poultry, & Fish

- Use good-quality meat. If you plan to can game or fish that you have caught or meat that you have harvested, refer to your county extension service or other qualified organization for tips on how to properly field dress, bleed, clean, and age the carcass.

- Chill meat to 40° or lower as soon as possible. If you aren't able to can the meat within a few days of slaughter, freeze it and keep frozen until ready to process. If you have bought the meat fresh at the store, follow these same guidelines.

- Trim off gristle, bruised spots, and fat from the meat before canning. Taking care during this stage will result in a milder-tasting product. Also, too much fat left on the meat can cause sealing failures.

- Only use a pressure canner—a water-bath canner is not safe when processing low-acid foods such as meat.

- Always use a trusted and tested canning recipe so you are confident the jars of meat have been processed for the correct amount of time.

- Take time to carefully read all instructions and make adjustments in psi according to your altitude. Refer to the altitude adjustment directions below.

- Have your dial gauge tested annually so you are certain that it's reading correctly.

- Vent your pressure canner for a full 10 minutes before setting the weight on the vent stem or closing the petcock to begin building pressure.

- Do not use a thickening agent such as flour or cornstarch when canning meat. If you want a thickened sauce or gravy, you can add them when you are preparing your meal.

- If you suspect spoilage when you open a jar, do not taste the contents. Instead, place the opened jars on their sides in a very large pot and cover with water; add the lids as well. Wash your hands carefully and then cover the pot and heat the contents to boiling. Boil for 30 minutes to help detoxify the food; cool and discard. When you are done, thoroughly scrub your hands and arms, all utensils and containers, counters, sink, and anything else that might have come in contact with the food.

- Clean the outside of the jars when processing is complete and the jars have cooled. Using a vinegar and water solution will help cut the grease that has migrated to the outside of the jars during processing

How To Prepare And Process Meat, Poultry, & Fish

In this section you will find listed the most common meats suitable for canning and the specific guidelines for each.

Altitude Adjustment Directions

Depending on the altitude where you are canning, you may need to adjust the psi of your canner in order to ensure that your food has been safely processed at the required high temperatures. The following chart lists the adjustments you need to make depending on where you live: Weighted gauge canner: Process at 10 pounds pressure from sea level to 1,000 feet in altitude; at 15 pounds pressure above 1,000 feet.

Dial gauge canner: Process at 11 pounds pressure from sea level to 2,000 feet in altitude; at 12 pounds pressure from 2,001 to 4,000 feet; at 13 pounds pressure from 4,001 to 6,000 feet; at 14 pounds pressure from 6,001 to 8,000 feet.

Ground Meat (Or Finely Chopped)

Bear, Beef, Elk, Lamb, Pork, Sausage, Venison

Note: If you decide to season your sausage before canning it, omit sage, which turns bitter and off-flavor when canned. You can always add sage later when you are preparing the food for eating. If your sausage is in casings, remove the meat from the casings before browning and canning.

When grinding venison, many people choose to add 1 part pork or beef fat for every 4 parts venison because the meat is naturally very lean.

You can shape your ground meat into patties (make sure they fit inside the jar) or meatballs, or simply leave as is. No matter which style you decide on, lightly brown the meat and then drain off fat. Fill jars with the meat; add boiling broth, tomato juice, or water, leaving 1-inch headspace. Add salt, if desired (1 tsp. per quart, ½ tsp. per pint). Following the pressure canning directions in chapter 4, process pints for 75 minutes and quarts for 90 minutes at 10 psi, adjusting the psi as necessary for your altitude according to the altitude adjustment directions.

Chunks, Cubes, / Strips

Bear, Beef, Elk, Lamb, Pork, Venison

You can reduce the heavy game flavor of venison and elk by removing large bones and then soaking the meat for 1 hour in a brine solution consisting of 1 tablespoon salt per quart of water. Rinse before processing.

Hot Pack: Partially precook meat by roasting, stewing, or browning in a small amount of fat until almost done. Drain off any fat that appears. Fill jars with the meat; add boiling broth, tomato juice, or water, leaving 1-inch headspace. (Tomato juice is especially good with wild game.) Add salt, if desired (1 tsp. per quart, ½ tsp. per pint). Following the pressure canning directions in chapter 4, process pints for 75 minutes and quarts for 90 minutes at 10 psi, adjusting the psi as necessary for your altitude according to the altitude adjustment directions.

Raw Pack: Fill jars with raw meat pieces, leaving 1-inch headspace. Add salt, if desired (1 tsp. per quart, ½ tsp. per pint). Do not add liquid. Following the pressure canning directions in chapter 4, process pints for 75 minutes and quarts for 90 minutes at 10 psi, adjusting the psi as necessary for your altitude according to the altitude adjustment directions.

Beef Broth (Stock)

Preparing broth: Crack trimmed beef bones, rinse, and put them in a large pot, adding water to cover. Bring to a boil, reduce heat, cover the pot, and simmer for 3 to 4 hours. Remove bones; when cool, pick off meat and set meat aside. Cool broth and skim off fat as it forms on top; strain broth, if desired. Combine the meat and broth and reheat to boiling. Fill jars, leaving 1-inch headspace. Add salt, if desired (1 tsp. per quart, ½ tsp. per pint). Following the pressure canning directions in chapter 4, process pints for 20 minutes and quarts for 25 minutes at 10 psi, adjusting the psi as necessary for your altitude according to the altitude adjustment directions.

Chicken, Rabbit, & Squirrel

Whenever possible, choose freshly killed and dressed animals. Soak dressed game for 1 hour in a brine solution made by dissolving 1 tablespoon salt for each quart of water used. Rinse.

Larger chickens are more flavorful than fryers; these are sometimes called stewing chickens. If hot-packing chicken, cook the bird with the skin on for more flavor, but take care to skim off excess fat before canning.

Cut the chicken, rabbit, or squirrel into sizes that will fit inside the jars. Remove excess fat. You can remove the bones if desired, but it's not necessary.

Hot Pack: Boil, steam, sauté, or roast meat until almost done. Fill jars with the meat; add boiling broth or water, leaving 1-inch headspace. Add salt, if desired (1 tsp. per quart, ½ tsp. per pint). Following the pressure canning directions in chapter 4, process as follows:

Without bones: pints 75 minutes; quarts 90 minutes at 10 psi, adjusting the psi as necessary for your altitude according to the altitude adjustment directions.

With bones: pints, 65 minutes; quarts 75 minutes at 10 psi, adjusting the psi as necessary for your altitude according to the altitude adjustment directions.

Raw Pack: Add salt, if desired (1 tsp. per quart, ½ tsp. per pint). Fill jars loosely with meat, leaving 1 inch headspace; do not add liquid. Following the pressure canning directions in chapter 4, process as follows:

Without bones: pints, 75 minutes; quarts 90 minutes at 10 psi, adjusting the psi as necessary for your altitude according to the altitude adjustment directions.

With bones: pints, 65 minutes; quarts 75 minutes at 10 psi, adjusting the psi as necessary for your altitude according to the altitude adjustment directions.

Chicken / Turkey Broth (Stock)

Place carcass in a large pot, adding water to cover. If desired, you can add a bouquet garni, celery, onion, and/or carrots for added flavor. Bring to a boil, reduce heat, cover the pot, and simmer for several hours (a large turkey carcass will take more time than a small chicken carcass). Remove carcass and bones and allow to cool enough to handle; pick meat off bones. Cool broth and skim off fat as it appears on top; strain broth, if desired. Combine meat and broth and reheat to boiling.

Fill jars, leaving 1-inch headspace. Add salt, if desired (1 tsp. per quart, ½ tsp. per pint). Following the pressure canning directions in chapter 4, process pints for 20 minutes and quarts for 25 minutes at 10 psi, adjusting the psi as necessary for your altitude according to the altitude adjustment directions.

Clams (Whole / Minced)

Keep clams alive until ready to process. Scrub shells and then steam clams to open. Toss any that don't open. Remove clams from cooking juice and save the juice. Remove meat from shells and then wash meat in a brine solution of 3 tablespoons salt dissolved in 1 gallon of water. Drain.

Next, blanch meat: combine 2 tablespoons lemon juice in a gallon of water; bring to a boil and then add the meat and boil for 2 minutes; drain.

At this point, you can mince the clam meat, if desired, using a knife, coarse grinder, or food processor.

Return the reserved cooking juice to a boil. (This will be used to pack jars for processing.) Pack clam meat into half-pint or pint jars (do not use quart jars), leaving 1-inch headspace. If using minced clam meat, pack loosely (about ¾ cup in half-pint jars or 1½ cups in pint jars). Add boiling cooking juice; if you run out of cooking juice, you can add boiling water to obtain the 1-inch headspace.

Following the pressure canning directions in chapter 4, process half-pints for 60 minutes and pints for 70 minutes at 10 psi, adjusting the psi as necessary for your altitude according to the altitude adjustment directions.

Crab

Keep crabs alive and on ice until ready to process.

In a large pot, bring ¼ cup bottled lemon juice and 2 tablespoons salt per gallon of water used to a boil; boil crabs for 20 minutes (if boiling more than 3 or 4 crabs at one time, you may need to lengthen cooking time a bit). Remove crabs from pot and cool in cold water; about 10 minutes.

When cool enough to handle, remove backs and clean crabs. Next, remove crabmeat and place the meat in a cool brine rinse solution of 2 tablespoons salt and 1 cup bottled lemon juice per gallon of water used for 2 minutes. Remove crabmeat and gently squeeze to remove excess rinse solution.

Pack crabmeat loosely (about ¾ cup in half-pint jars or 1½ cups in pint jars—do not use quart jars), leaving 1-inch headspace. In each jar, add either vinegar or lemon juice as follows:

Half-pint jars: 1½ tsps. vinegar or 2 tablespoons bottled lemon juice

Pint jars: 1 tablespoon vinegar or 4 tablespoons bottled lemon juice Add boiling water to cover, leaving 1-inch headspace. Following the pressure canning directions in chapter 4, process half-pints and pints for 80 minutes at 10 psi, adjusting the psi as necessary for your altitude according to the altitude adjustment directions.

Fish

(For Tuna, See Recipe Below)

Use only fresh-caught fish that was cleaned soon after catching and kept chilled until ready to process. Soak the fish for one hour in a brine solution made of 1 cup salt dissolved in 1 gallon of water. Drain well. Pack fish into hot half-pint or pint jars (do not use quarts), skin side out, leaving 1-inch headspace.

Following the pressure canning directions in chapter 4, process half-pints and pints for 100 minutes at 10 psi, adjusting the psi as necessary for your altitude according to the altitude adjustment directions.

Oysters

Keep oysters alive and cool until ready to process. Wash shells well. Steam or bake to open and then quickly cool them; remove meat.

Wash meat in a brine solution using ½ cup salt per each gallon of water used. Drain.

Pack meat into half-pint or pint jars (do not use quarts), leaving 1-inch headspace. Cover with boiling water, again leaving 1-inch headspace. Following the pressure canning directions in chapter 4, process half-pints and pints for 75 minutes at 10 psi, adjusting the psi as necessary for your altitude according to the altitude adjustment directions.

Shrimp

Remove heads immediately after catching; keep shrimp chilled until ready to process. Wash and drain shrimp.

In a large pot, make a brine solution using 1 cup salt, 1 cup vinegar, and 1 gallon water; bring to a boil and then add shrimp. Boil shrimp for 8 to 10 minutes; drain. Rinse in cold water and then peel shrimp.

Make another brine solution, which will be used to pack jars, using 1 to 3 tablespoons salt for each gallon of water. Bring to a boil.

Pack half-pint or pint jars (don't use quarts) with shrimp, leaving 1-inch headspace. Cover with the boiling brine, again leaving 1-inch headspace. Following the pressure canning directions in chapter 4, process half-pints and pints for 45 minutes at 10 psi, adjusting the psi as necessary for your altitude according to the altitude adjustment directions.

Tuna

The trick to canning sweet-tasting tuna is in the preparation. After skinning, removing viscera, bleeding the fish, and deboning, take extra care in the final cleaning to remove all dark flesh, blood vessels, and membranes. Rinse well. The cleaner your meat is, the better it will taste once canned, so take your time and do a thorough job.

Also, you can pack your tuna either precooked or raw. Precooking removes some of the oils present in the tuna, and some people believe this helps remove strong flavor. But it's easier to can raw tuna, and if you have done a good job cleaning the fish, strong flavor won't be a problem.

To Precook: Place the cleaned tuna on a rack in a large baking pan. Bake at 225° to 250°F for 2½ to 4 hours, depending on size of fish. Alternatively, you can bake the fish at 350° for 1 hour. You can also steam the tuna for 2 to 4 hours. It's done when the internal temperature reaches about 170°. Refrigerate tuna overnight to firm the flesh before canning.

Canning Precooked Tuna: Pack precooked tuna into half-pint or pint jars (do not use quarts), pressing down gently and leaving 1-inch headspace. For half-pint jars, add ½ tsp. salt and 1 to 3 tablespoons vegetable oil, water, or a combination of oil and water; for pint jars, add 1 tsp. salt and 2 to 6 tablespoons vegetable oil, water, or a combination of oil and water. Following the pressure canning directions in chapter 4, process half-pints and pints for 100 minutes at 10 psi, adjusting the psi as necessary for your altitude according to the altitude adjustment directions.

Canning Raw Tuna: Pack raw tuna into half-pint or pint jars (do not use quarts), pressing down to fill in the space inside the jar and leaving 1-inch headspace. You can add water to cover, again leaving 1-inch headspace, but this isn't necessary as it's safe to can the raw tuna with no added liquid. Add salt, if desired. Following the pressure canning directions in chapter 4, process half-pints and pints for 100 minutes at 10 psi, adjusting the psi as necessary for your altitude according to the altitude adjustment directions.

Chapter 12: Soups, Stews, & Other Good Things

While this chapter will give you plenty of recipes for all sorts of canned goods that use more than one ingredient, you may be surprised to notice what isn't included here. That's because as testing and research continue over time, safety guidelines change. So what used to be considered perfectly safe—for example, pumpkin pie filling or beef barley stew thickened with flour or cornstarch—today might be considered risky. The best way to deal with these changing canning guidelines is to make sure your recipes are up-to-date and to follow sound recipes.

Unfortunately, this could very well mean that a favorite recipe that you or someone you know has used for many years won't pass the safety test. It's also likely that at some point you'll hear someone say they don't care about the latest canning guidelines because they've been using their recipes for years and years and "no one's gotten sick yet." And they are no doubt right because the incidence of home-canned food causing food-borne illness is almost nonexistent. Even so, I urge you to use only those canning recipes that you know are safe. Because when it comes to our families, why take chances?

That being said, you can devise your own recipes or tweak a favorite recipe you already use. Just make sure there are no unsafe foods present and look up each individual ingredient you've used when deciding how long to process. The processing time for your canner load will be for whichever ingredient needs the longest amount of time. So next time you make spaghetti sauce or a pot of soup for supper, make plenty and can the leftovers. By adding to your pantry shelves a bit at a time this way, you'll soon have a full larder of good meals just waiting to be heated and eaten. What a good feeling that is!

Here's a list of some foods that you should not can:

- Fats, including mayonnaise, lard, oil (except for a small amount included in a recipe), butter, fatty cuts of meat (trim the fat)

- Dairy, including milk, cheese, sour cream, whipping cream, yogurt, buttermilk, tofu, soy or coconut milk, etc.

- Eggs

- Grains, including oats, wheat, rice, barley, cornmeal, bread

- Pasta and noodles

- Mashed vegetables and meats (mashed potatoes, pumpkin pie filling, liver pâté, etc.), giblets, pureed soups

- Thickeners, including flour, tapioca, cornstarch, cornmeal, and arrowroot.

Note: Clear Jel is a modified cornstarch product that can be used in canned jams, jellies, and pie filling as it doesn't tend to break down when exposed to the high heat needed to can the fruit.

- Creamy dishes, including pudding, refried beans (instead, mash them when you remove from jar to heat and eat), peanut butter, pesto

- Sage (this is one herb that turns bitter-tasting when canned)
- Dry beans that have not been previously soaked (to reduce phytic acid levels) and then partially cooked before canning

Altitude Adjustment Directions

Depending on the altitude where you are canning, you may need to adjust the psi of your canner in order to ensure that your food has been safely processed at the required high temperatures. The following chart lists the adjustments you need to make depending on where you live: Weighted gauge canner: Process at 10 pounds pressure from sea level to 1,000 feet in altitude; at 15 pounds pressure above 1,000 feet.

Dial gauge canner: Process at 11 pounds pressure from sea level to 2,000 feet in altitude; at 12 pounds pressure from 2,001 to 4,000 feet; at 13 pounds pressure from 4,001 to 6,000 feet; at 14 pounds pressure from 6,001 to 8,000 feet.

Baked Beans

- 8 lbs. navy beans (about 16 cups dry beans)
- 4½ quarts tomato juice
- 2⅓ cups brown sugar (1 lb.)
- ½ tsp. pepper
- 1 T. ground mustard
- 4 cups cooked ham, diced
- 8 T. salt
- 1 cup molasses
- 2 T. vinegar
- 1 T. cinnamon (optional)

Preparing

Place beans in a large pot and add water to cover; bring to a boil, cover, remove from heat, and let set for 1 hour; drain.

Return beans to pot, add fresh water to cover, and cook them until they are almost done; drain. Return the beans to the large pot and keep warm.

In a large saucepan, mix together the other ingredients and simmer, stirring, for 3 minutes; add sauce to the beans and mix thoroughly. If mixture seems too thick or too dry, you can add some boiling water or tomato juice to get a consistency that seems right to you. Heat bean mixture thoroughly to simmering and then ladle into jars, leaving 1-inch headspace. Following the pressure canning directions in chapter 4, process quarts for 70 minutes and pints for 65 minutes at 10 psi, adjusting the psi as necessary for your altitude according to the altitude adjustment directions. Makes about 14 quarts.

Baked Beans, (Boston Style)

- 5 lbs. navy beans (about 10 cups dry beans)
- 3 T. molasses
- 1 T. vinegar
- 2 tsp. salt
- ½ tsp. pepper
- 1 tsp. powdered mustard
- 2 T. Worcestershire sauce
- ¼ cup brown sugar
- 3 slices bacon, cut into 1-inch pieces

Preparing

Put dry beans in a large pot and add enough water to cover by 2 inches. Bring to a boil; turn off heat, cover, and let set for one hour. Drain.

Place the drained beans back in the large pot and add fresh water to cover. Bring to a boil and boil for 5 minutes; drain, this time reserving the cooking liquid.

In a large saucepan, mix together the molasses, vinegar, salt, pepper, powdered mustard, Worcestershire sauce, and brown sugar, plus 5 cups of the reserved cooking liquid from the beans (save the remainder of the liquid to be used during baking—see below). Heat to boiling; turn off heat and let set while you prepare the beans for baking.

In a large Dutch oven or heavy casserole dish, mix together the beans and bacon. Pour on the sauce, carefully mixing with the beans. Bake the beans in a 350° oven, covered, for 3 to 4 hours, adding cooking liquid from the beans as needed to keep the baking beans from drying out. If you run out of cooking liquid, you can use boiling water if needed.

Fill hot jars with the hot baked beans, leaving 1-inch headspace. Top off jars with boiling water so beans are fully submerged, keeping the headspace. Following the pressure canning directions in chapter 4, process quarts for 75 minutes and pints for 65 minutes at 10 psi, adjusting the psi as necessary for your altitude according to the altitude adjustment directions. Makes about 7 quarts.

Barbeque Sauce

- 10 quarts tomatoes, peeled, cored, and chopped
- 1 quart onions, chopped
- 6 cloves garlic, minced
- 1½ T. hot pepper flakes
- 2 T. celery seeds
- 3 cups brown sugar
- 2 cups 5% vinegar
- ⅔ cup lemon juice
- 4 T. salt
- 3 T. nutmeg or mace

- 2 T. mustard powder
- 2 tsp. ginger
- 2 tsp. cinnamon

Preparing

In a large pot, mix together the tomatoes, onions, garlic, pepper flakes, and celery seeds. Bring to a boil, stirring constantly; reduce heat, cover, and simmer until tomatoes and onions are soft, about 30 minutes. Run tomato mixture through a food mill, sieve, or strainer (such as Victorio) to extract the juice and the pulp.

Place pulp and juice in a pot and add the brown sugar, vinegar, lemon juice, salt, nutmeg, mustard powder, ginger, and cinnamon. Bring to a boil, reduce heat, and simmer for about 30 minutes, stirring frequently, until the mixture is thickened.

Ladle hot barbeque sauce into hot pint or half-pint jars, leaving ½-inch headspace. Process half-pints and pints in a boiling water canner for 20 minutes at 0 to 1,000 feet, 25 minutes at 1,001 to 6,000 feet, or 30 minutes at 6001 to 8,000 feet. Makes about 6 pints.

Bean Soup

- 6 cups dried navy beans
- 1 large ham hock or ½ lb. salt pork
- 1½ cups onion, chopped
- 1 hot red pepper, minced
- Salt and pepper to taste

Preparing

Place beans in a large pot and cover with water by at least 2 inches. Bring beans to a boil and boil 2 minutes; cover pot and let set for 1 hour; drain.

Cover beans with fresh water and add meat, onion, and pepper. Bring to a boil, cover, and simmer for 2 hours or until beans are tender. Remove ham hock from pot and when cool enough to handle, cut meat from bone. Dice the meat and set aside.

With a potato masher, coarsely mash beans in the liquid (don't drain!). Return diced meat to soup and heat through.

Ladle hot soup into hot jars, leaving 1-inch headspace. Following the pressure canning directions in chapter 4, process quarts for 90 minutes and pints for 75 minutes at 10 psi, adjusting the psi as necessary for your altitude according to the altitude adjustment directions. Makes about 6 quarts or 12 pints.

Beef Stew With Vegetables

- 4 lbs. beef stew meat (any cut will work)
- 3 cups onions, chopped
- 8 cups carrots, sliced
- 3 cups celery, chopped
- 12 cups potatoes, peeled and chunked
- 10 cups broth or water
- ½ tsp. summer savory (optional)
- Salt and pepper to taste

Preparing

Brown meat in a large Dutch oven or pot. Add onions and sauté until onions are soft. Add remaining ingredients and bring to a boil. Ladle stew, including broth, into jars, leaving 1-inch headspace. Following the pressure canning directions in chapter 4, process quarts for 90 minutes and pints for 75 minutes at 10 psi, adjusting the psi as necessary for your altitude according to the altitude adjustment directions. Makes about 7 quarts.

Black Bean Soup

- 6 cups dried black beans
- 3 onions, chopped
- 10 cloves garlic, minced
- 2 T. cumin
- 2 T. salt
- 1 tsp. black pepper
- 1 tsp. cayenne pepper
- 3½ cups orange juice
- 4 cups beef or vegetable broth
- 4 cups water
- 4 carrots, diced
- 2 bell peppers (red or green or combination), diced
- 2 sweet potatoes, peeled and diced
- 5 tomatoes, skinned, seeded, and chopped

Preparing

Put dried beans in a large pot; add water to cover by 1 to 2 inches, cover pot, and soak overnight. Drain.

Put drained beans in a large pot; add fresh water to cover. Bring to a boil, reduce heat, and simmer for 30 minutes. Drain. Keep warm.

Combine remaining ingredients in another large pot. Bring to a boil and boil gently for 5 minutes.

Divide black beans equally between 6 quart jars. Ladle hot soup broth (including vegetables) over the beans, leaving 1-inch headspace. Following the pressure canning directions in chapter 4, process quarts for 90 minutes and pints for 75 minutes at 10 psi, adjusting the psi as necessary for your altitude according to the altitude adjustment directions. Makes about 6 quarts.

Butternut Squash Soup

Note: This is the soup base recipe. Following the recipe are instructions for using the soup base to make creamy butternut squash soup.

- 5 lbs. butternut squash, peeled and cut into ½-inch cubes
- 2½ lbs. red potatoes, peeled and cut into ½-inch cubes
- 5 stalks celery, coarsely chopped
- 5 carrots, coarsely chopped
- 3 onions, chopped
- 2 T. salt

Preparing

Place prepared squash and potatoes in a large pot. Add water to cover; bring to a boil and boil for 2 minutes; drain and return squash mixture to pot. Add remainder of ingredients and gently mix.

Pack hot squash mix into hot jars, leaving 1-inch headspace. Ladle boiling water over the vegetables, again leaving 1-inch headspace. Following the pressure canning directions in chapter 4, process quarts for 90 minutes and pints for 60 minutes at 10 psi, adjusting the psi as necessary for your altitude according to the altitude adjustment directions. Makes about 5 quarts.

To serve: Drain squash mixture. Puree in a blender (soup will be very smooth), or mash with a potato masher (soup will be lumpy). Add about 1 cup milk or cream to the soup and heat thoroughly. Add spices if desired—try nutmeg, ginger, curry, or parsley. Top individual servings of squash soup with a dollop of sour cream.

Carrot And Fennel Soup

- 2 fennel bulbs, sliced thin
- 1 T. olive oil
- 4 lbs. carrots, peeled and sliced
- 6 cups vegetable or beef broth
- 6 cups water
- ½ tsp. pepper
- salt to taste (optional)

Preparing

Sauté fennel in olive oil until transparent; blot fennel to remove excess oil.

In a large pot combine fennel, carrots, broth, and water. Bring to a boil; reduce heat and simmer for about 45 minutes, stirring occasionally. Mash soup mixture using a potato masher; there will still be food bits.

Ladle hot soup into hot jars, leaving 1-inch headspace. Following the pressure canning directions in chapter 4, process pints and quarts for 35 minutes at 10 psi, adjusting the psi as necessary for your altitude according to the altitude adjustment directions. Makes about 6 quarts.

Note: If you want creamier soup, when you are ready to heat and serve, you can puree soup in a blender before heating. You can also add a dollop of sour cream on each serving for a nice touch

Chicken Corn Soup

- 3–4 lbs. stewing chicken, or pieces
- 1½ gallons water
- 2 bay leaves
- ½ tsp. thyme
- salt and pepper to taste
- 3 quarts corn, fresh, frozen, or canned

Preparing

In a large pot combine the chicken, water, bay leaves, thyme, and salt and pepper.

Bring to a boil, cover, and simmer until chicken is cooked through and tender, about 1½ to 2 hours. Remove chicken and cut meat off bones; dice meat into bite-sized pieces. Remove bay leaves and skim fat off the top of the broth. Return diced meat to the broth and add corn. Simmer soup for about 5 minutes or until corn is heated through.

Ladle hot soup into hot jars, filling jars about halfway with chicken and corn, and then filling the jars to the top with broth, leaving 1-inch headspace. Following the pressure canning directions in chapter 4, process quarts for 90 minutes and pints for 75 minutes at 10 psi, adjusting the psi as necessary for your altitude according to the altitude adjustment directions. Makes about 10 quarts.

Chicken Soup

- 5 quarts chicken broth or stock
- 3 cups diced cooked chicken

- 1½ cups celery, diced
- 1½ cups carrots, sliced
- 1 cup onion, diced
- Salt and pepper to taste

Preparing

Note: This recipe has a lot of broth, which makes it perfect for making chicken noodle soup. When ready to serve, simply cook a handful of noodles right in the soup (which will thicken the soup somewhat) or cook the noodles separately and then add them to the hot soup. Also good with cooked rice.

Combine broth, chicken, celery, carrots, and onion in a large pot and bring to a boil. Reduce heat and simmer for 30 minutes. Season with salt and pepper to taste.

Ladle hot soup into hot jars, leaving 1-inch headspace. Following the pressure canning directions in chapter 4, process quarts for 90 minutes and pints for 75 minutes at 10 psi, adjusting the psi as necessary for your altitude according to the altitude adjustment directions. Makes about 6 quarts.

Chicken Stew

- 4 lbs. chicken pieces, or 1 large stewing chicken
- 5 cups chicken stock (saved from boiling the chicken pieces)
- 1 28-oz. can diced tomatoes, drained (or use 2 quarts home-canned tomatoes, drained)
- 3 large potatoes, peeled and cubed (about ½ inch)
- 2 cups onion, chopped
- 5 carrots, peeled and cut into 2-inch lengths (half the lengths also if they are big in diameter)
- 3 celery ribs, chopped
- 2 cups butter beans or lima beans (fresh or frozen)
- 2 cups corn (fresh or frozen)
- 2 bay leaves

- ½ tsp. rosemary
- 1 tsp. thyme
- 1 tsp. cayenne pepper
- ½ tsp. black pepper
- 3 cloves garlic, minced
- 1 cup okra (optional)

Preparing

Place chicken in a large pot and add water to cover. Bring to a boil and reduce heat, cover, and simmer until chicken is cooked and tender, about 1½ hours. Remove meat from bones and cut into large bite-size pieces. Skim off fat from broth; measure out and save 5 cups broth.

Return skimmed broth to pot; add the vegetables and simmer for about 15 minutes or until vegetables are heated through and just beginning to soften. Return chicken to pot and add okra if using. Continue to simmer for about 5 more minutes.

Pack hot stew into hot jars, leaving 1-inch headspace. Following the pressure canning directions in chapter 4, process quarts for 90 minutes and pints for 75 minutes at 10 psi, adjusting the psi as necessary for your altitude according to the altitude adjustment directions. Makes about 6 quarts.

Chili Con Carne

- 4½ cups dried pinto or kidney beans
- 2 quarts water for soaking beans
- 4 to 5 lbs. ground beef
- 2 cups onions, chopped
- 1½ cups peppers, chopped (bell or hot)
- 4 tsp. salt
- 1½ tsp. black pepper
- 4 to 6 tsp. chili powder
- 3 quarts crushed or whole canned tomatoes

Preparing

Cover beans with 2 quarts water, cover, and let soak in the refrigerator or a cool place for about 12 hours. Drain. Add fresh water to cover; cook for 30 minutes; drain.

In a large pot, brown ground beef, onions, and peppers if using; drain off fat. Add salt, black pepper, chili powder, tomatoes, and drained cooked beans. Bring mixture to a boil and simmer for 5 minutes.

Pack hot into hot jars, leaving 1-inch headspace. Following the pressure canning directions in chapter 4, process quarts for 90 minutes and pints for 75 minutes at 10 psi, adjusting the psi as necessary for your altitude according to the altitude adjustment directions. Makes about 6 to 7 quarts.

Clam Chowder

Note: Milk and butter are not part of this recipe as those ingredients are not safe to can. Milk and butter are added when ready to serve the chowder (see below for directions).

- ½ lb. salt pork, diced
- 1 cup onion, chopped
- 3 to 4 quarts cleaned chopped clams in juice
- 2 quarts potatoes, peeled and diced
- 2 quarts boiling water

- Salt and pepper to taste

Preparing

In a large pot brown the salt pork and drain off fat. Add onion and cook until tender. Add clams with their juice, potatoes, and boiling water; boil for 10 minutes. Season to taste with salt and pepper.

Ladle hot chowder into half-pint or pint jars (do not use quarts), leaving 1-inch headspace. Following the pressure canning directions in chapter 4, process half- pints and pints for 100 minutes at 10 psi, adjusting the psi as necessary for your altitude according to the altitude adjustment directions. Makes about 10 pints.

To serve chowder: For every 1 pint of chowder used, add 2 tablespoons butter and 2 cups milk. Place all ingredients in a saucepan and heat through.

Cranberry Sauce

- 4 cups sugar
- 4 cups water

- 8 cups fresh cranberries
- Grated zest of 1 orange (optional)

Preparing

In a large pot, mix together sugar and water; bring to a boil while stirring to dissolve sugar. Turn heat to high and boil hard for 5 minutes. Add cranberries and return to a boil; reduce heat and boil gently, stirring often, until cranberries burst and the sauce begins to sheet off a metal spoon (takes about 15 minutes of boiling time). Add the orange zest if using.

Ladle hot cranberry sauce into hot pint or half-pint jars, leaving ¼-inch headspace. Process half-pints and pints in a boiling water canner for 15 minutes at 0 to 1,000 feet, 20 minutes at 1,001 to 6,000 feet, or 25 minutes at 6,001 to 8,000 feet. Makes about 4 to 5 pints.

Farmer's Soup

- 2 lbs. hamburger
- 2 large onions, chopped
- 2 cups celery, chopped

- 3 cups potatoes, cut into 1-inch cubes
- 2 cups carrots, sliced
- Salt and pepper to taste
- 1 quart tomato sauce
- 5 quarts water or beef broth
- Brown hamburger and onion; drain fat.

Preparing

In a large pot, combine browned meat mixture with remaining ingredients. Bring to a boil and simmer for several minutes, just until vegetables begin to soften.

Pack hot soup into hot jars, filling each jar about halfway with food pieces and filling to the top of the jar with the cooking broth, leaving 1-inch headspace. Following the pressure canning directions in chapter 4, process quarts for 75 minutes and pints for 60 minutes at 10 psi, adjusting the psi as necessary for your altitude according to the altitude adjustment directions. Makes about 7 quarts.

To serve: This soup is good served heated as is. But it's extra tasty if you mix 3 tablespoons cornmeal with ¼ cup cold water and stir the mixture into your hot soup; continue heating and stirring soup for several more minutes or until soup is thickened slightly.

Green Tomatillo Salsa

- 5 cups tomatillos, peeled and chopped
- 1½ cups Anaheim chilies, seeded and skinned (see below for instructions on how to skin them)
- ½ cup jalapeno peppers, seeded and chopped
- 4 cups onion, peeled and chopped
- 1½ cups lemon juice
- 6 cloves garlic, minced
- 1 T. ground cumin (or you can use finely chopped fresh cilantro)
- 3 T. oregano leaves (not ground)
- 2 T. salt
- 1 tsp. black pepper

Preparing

To skin the Anaheim chilies, you will need to char the skins, allow them to steam so the skins loosen, and then rub the skins off the chilies. To char, you can place the chilies on a roasting pan and then broil them in the oven, turning them as they char so all surfaces get blackened; or you can use a backyard grill and char them over the open flame, making sure to turn them so they are completely charred. Once the chilies are charred, immediately put them between two damp towels or place in a paper bag and close up the top. Allow them to steam for about 10 minutes. Next, remove them from their steamer container and—using gloves!—rub the skins. They should slip right off. For bits that want to adhere to the chili, use a sharp knife to remove those areas.

Don't make the mistake of thinking that you can get away with not using gloves when working with hot peppers. I learned this painful lesson the hard way, and I don't advise it!

Mix all ingredients in a large pot and, stirring frequently, bring mixture to a boil. Reduce heat and simmer for 20 minutes, stirring enough so that the bottom doesn't scorch.

Fill pint jars with the hot salsa, leaving ½-inch headspace. Process pints in a boiling water canner for 15 minutes at 0 to 1,000 feet, 20 minutes at 1,001 to

6,000 feet, or 25 minutes at 6,001 to 8000 feet. Makes about 4 pints.

Hamburger Stew

- 3 lbs. hamburger (need about 6 cups browned meat)
- 2 quarts green beans, strings removed and snapped into 1½-inch pieces
- 3 quarts potatoes, peeled and cut into 1½-inch cubes
- Salt and pepper to taste

Preparing

In a large pot, brown hamburger and drain grease. Add green beans, potatoes, and salt and pepper; add enough water or beef broth to cover; bring to a boil and simmer for about 5 minutes.

Ladle hot stew into hot jars, leaving 1-inch headspace. If necessary, top off jars with boiling broth or water, maintaining the 1-inch headspace. Following the pressure canning directions in chapter 4, process pints for 75 minutes and quarts for 90 minutes at 10 psi, adjusting the psi as necessary for your altitude according to the altitude adjustment directions. Makes about 7 quarts.

Hot Dog Green Tomato Relish

- 3 quarts chopped green tomatoes
- 3 onions, chopped
- 3 green peppers (bell), chopped (or use 2 green and 1 red bell pepper)
- 6 T. salt
- 3 cups sugar
- 3 T. prepared mustard
- 3 tsp. celery salt
- 10 whole cloves
- 3 cups 5% vinegar

Preparing

In a large bowl, combine tomatoes, onions, and peppers; add salt and mix well to combine; let set for 1 hour; drain.

In a large pot combine the drained vegetables, sugar, mustard, and celery salt. Tie whole cloves in a cheesecloth or spice bag and add to vegetables. Stir in vinegar. Over medium-low heat, bring mixture to a simmer and cook, stirring occasionally, for 20 minutes; remove spice bag.

Ladle hot relish into hot half-pint or pint jars, leaving ¼-inch headspace. Process pints and half-pints in a boiling water canner for 10 minutes at 0 to 1,000 feet; 15 minutes at 1,001 ot 3,000 feet; 20 minutes at 3,001 to 6,000 feet; 25 minutes at 6,001 to 8,000 feet; 30 minutes above 8,000 feet. Makes about 7 pints.

Lamb Stew

- 2 lbs. red potatoes, peeled and cubed
- 3 lbs. lamb, cut into 1½-inch cubes
- 3 onions, chunked
- 8 cloves garlic, minced

- 4 quarts beef broth
- 1 quart water
- 4 T. rosemary leaves
- 4 T. thyme
- 3 bay leaves
- 4 T. salt
- 4 tsp. black pepper
- 12 carrots, peeled and sliced

Preparing

In a large pot, mix together all ingredients.

Bring to a boil, reduce heat, and simmer for 20 minutes. Pack hot stew into hot jars, filling about halfway with food pieces. Ladle the cooking broth over the stew, leaving 1-inch headspace. Following the pressure canning directions in chapter 4, process quarts for 90 minutes and pints for 75 minutes at 10 psi, adjusting the psi as necessary for your altitude according to the altitude adjustment directions. Makes about 7 quarts.

Mincemeat Pie Filling

- 2 cups suet, finely chopped
- 4 lbs. ground beef (can also use ground elk or venison)
- 5 quarts chopped apples
- 2 lbs. dark seedless raisins (about 5½ cups)
- 1 lb. white raisins (about 2¾ cups)
- 2 quarts apple cider
- 2 T. ground cinnamon
- 2 tsp. ground nutmeg
- 5 cups sugar
- 1 T. salt

Preparing

Simmer meat and suet in water until cooked. Peel, core, and quarter apples. Put meat, suet, and apples through a food grinder using a medium blade. Combine all ingredients in a large pot and simmer 1 hour or until slightly thickened, stirring often. Immediately fill quart jars, leaving 1-inch headspace. Following the pressure canning directions in chapter 4, process quarts for 90 minutes at 10 psi, adjusting the psi as necessary for your altitude according to the altitude adjustment directions. Makes about 7 quarts.

Minestrone Soup

- 1 cup dried white beans (Great Northern, navy, cannellini)
- 1 cup peeled, cubed potatoes
- 1 onion, chopped
- 4 cloves garlic, minced
- 3 carrots, peeled and cut into ½-inch lengths
- 2 lbs. tomatoes, skinned, cored, seeded, and chopped
- 3 cups green beans, cut into ½-inch lengths
- 1 cup spinach or kale, chopped
- 2 quarts chicken broth or stock
- 2 tsp. oregano
- 1 T. basil
- 1 T. salt
- 2 tsp. pepper

Preparing

In a pot, cover beans with enough water to cover by 1 to 2 inches; bring to a boil and boil for 2 minutes. Remove from heat and let beans soak for an hour; drain and rinse beans. Return beans to pot and cover with 2 quarts fresh water. Bring to a boil, reduce heat, and simmer beans for 30 minutes. Keep beans hot when done cooking.

While beans are cooking, prepare vegetables. Place prepared potatoes in one quart of cold water to which 1 tablespoon lemon juice has been added. (This will keep the potatoes from turning gray.) Cut the other vegetables and set aside. When ready to make soup, drain and quickly rinse potatoes.

Combine all ingredients except beans in a large pot. Bring to a boil, reduce heat, and then simmer for 10 minutes.

Drain beans and divide them between 7 quart jars. Using a slotted spoon, divide the vegetables between the jars. Next, ladle broth in equal portions between the 7 jars—you need 1-inch headspace, so if you run out of broth, top off each jar with some boiling water to get to the proper level. Following the pressure canning directions in chapter 4, process quarts for 90 minutes at 10 psi, adjusting the psi as necessary for your altitude according to the altitude adjustment directions. Makes about 7 quarts.

To serve: You can heat and eat as is, or you can add some cooked noodles to the minestrone. If you prefer, you can omit the spinach or kale from the canned soup recipe and add it to the soup when heating it up to serve instead. Top individual bowls with grated Parmesan cheese.

Mix-Your-Own Vegetable And Meat Soup

Note: You want to have half of each jar filled with meat and vegetables and then fill the jar to the top, leaving 1-inch headspace, with broth.

Meat Or Poultry: Boil meat in water to cover until cooked through and tender. Remove bones and chop meat.

Vegetables: Choose a variety of vegetables according to taste or what you have available.

Chop vegetables and boil in water to cover for several minutes, or until vegetables are barely cooked.

Dried Beans Or Peas: For each cup of dried beans or peas, add 3 cups of water. Bring to a boil and then boil for 2 minutes; remove from heat, cover pot, and let beans soak for 1 hour; drain. Cover with fresh water and reheat to boiling; drain.

Broth: You can use meat or poultry broth, canned tomatoes, water, or a combination.

Spices: Choose any spices that please your palette, but remember—sage should not be added during the canning process because it turns bitter. If you want sage in your soup, add some once you open the jar and heat it for serving.

Combine all prepared ingredients, making sure there is plenty of broth to cover the meat and vegetables. Bring soup to a boil, reduce heat, and simmer for 5 minutes.

Pack hot jars with hot soup, adding more hot broth as needed to fill the jars, leaving 1-inch headspace. Following the pressure canning directions in chapter 4, process quarts for 75 minutes and pints for 60 minutes at 10 psi, adjusting the psi as necessary for your altitude according to the altitude adjustment directions.

Pizza Sauce

- 25 to 30 good-sized tomatoes
- 2 large onions, finely diced
- 4 cloves garlic, minced
- 2 T. lemon juice
- 1 tsp. black pepper
- 2 T. parsley
- 1 T. each sugar, oregano, and basil
- 2 tsp. salt
- 1 tsp. each rosemary and celery seed
- ½ tsp. summer savory

Preparing

Sauté onions and garlic in a small amount of olive oil until soft. Blot oil with paper towels to remove excess. Put onion mixture in a large pot and set aside.

Scald tomatoes to remove skins by plunging them into boiling water for 30 to 45 seconds and then running them under cold water. Slip skins off to peel. Remove cores and seeds and finely chop. Place chopped tomatoes in the large pot with the onions and garlic; add remaining ingredients.

Cook on low heat, stirring regularly, until mixture is simmering; continue to cook until the mixture has been reduced by about half and is thick—about 1½ to 2 hours.

Ladle hot sauce into hot pint jars, leaving 1 inch headspace. Following the pressure canning directions in chapter 4, process pints for 20 minutes at 10 psi, adjusting the psi as necessary for your altitude according to the altitude adjustment directions. Makes about 4 to 5 pints.

Pork Stew

- 2 quarts pork, cut into 1½-inch cubes
- 2 quarts carrots, sliced
- 3 cups celery, chopped
- 3 cups onions, chopped

- 3 quarts potatoes, peeled and cubed
- 1½ T. salt
- 1 to 2 tsp. thyme
- ½ tsp. pepper
- Boiling water or broth

Preparing

In a large pot, brown the pork cubes in a small amount of vegetable oil.

In another large pot or saucepan place the carrots, celery, onions, and potatoes and add water to cover. Bring to a boil and simmer for 2 minutes; drain vegetables and add them to the large pot with the browned meat. Add seasonings and mix carefully but thoroughly, keeping the mixture hot. Pack the stew into hot jars, leaving 1-inch headspace. Ladle boiling water or broth over the stew, again leaving 1-inch headspace. Following the pressure canning directions in chapter 4, process quarts for 90 minutes and pints for 75 minutes at 10 psi, adjusting the psi as necessary for your altitude according to the altitude adjustment directions. Makes about 7 quarts.

Sandwich Spread

- 2 lbs. tomatoes
- 7 lbs. red bell peppers, minced
- 3 cloves garlic, minced
- ½ cup minced onion
- ¾ cup red wine vinegar or regular 5% vinegar
- 3 T. finely minced fresh basil
- 2 T. sugar
- 2 tsp. Salt

Preparing

Skin tomatoes by plunging them in boiling water for about 45 seconds or until skins begin to crack. Next, plunge them in ice cold water; when cool enough to handle, peel the skins; core and seed tomatoes and then finely chop them.

In a large pot, mix all ingredients together. On fairly low heat, stirring frequently so it doesn't scorch on the bottom of the pot, heat the mixture to boiling. Reduce heat and simmer for about 20 to 30 minutes or until the mixture thickens and mounds on a spoon.

Ladle hot sandwich spread into hot half-pint or pint jars, leaving ½-inch headspace. Following the water-bath canning directions in chapter 3, process half-pints and pints in a boiling water canner for 15 minutes at 0 to 1,000 feet; 20 minutes at 1,001 to 3,000 feet; 25 minutes at 3,001 to 6,000 feet; 30 minutes at 6,001 to 8,000 feet; 35 minutes above 8,000 feet. Makes about 4 pints.

South Of The Border Chicken Soup

- 3 boneless skinless chicken breasts, cooked and shredded or cubed
- 1½ cups carrots, sliced
- 2 cups celery, chopped
- 6 cups tomatoes, diced (fresh or canned)
- 4 to 6 jalapeno peppers, finely diced (fresh or canned), optional
- 2 cans kidney beans (15 ounces each)
- 12 cups chicken broth

- 3 cups corn (fresh or frozen)
- 1 tsp. ground cumin
- 1 T. salt
- 3 cloves garlic, minced

Preparing

In a large pot, bring all ingredients except cooked chicken to a boil; cover and simmer for 5 minutes. Add cooked chicken and continue to simmer until chicken is hot.

Ladle hot soup into jars, leaving 1-inch headspace. Following the directions in chapter 4, "Pressure Canning Guide," process quarts for 90 minutes and pints for 75 minutes at 10 psi, adjusting the psi as necessary for your altitude according to the altitude adjustment directions. Makes about 7 quarts.

Spicy Apple Plum Brown Sauce

- 2½ quarts apples, peeled, cored, and chopped
- 2½ quarts plums, pitted and chopped
- 5 cups onions, chopped

- 6 cups malt vinegar

- 5 cups sugar

- ½ cup salt

- ½ cup Worcestershire sauce

- 4 cloves, garlic, minced

- 2 tsp. ground ginger

- 2 tsp. ground nutmeg

- 2 tsp. ground allspice

- 2 tsp. cayenne pepper

Preparing

In a large pot, mix together all ingredients. On low heat, and stirring frequently, bring to a slow boil; reduce heat so mixture simmers, and cook, stirring often, for 3 to 4 hours or until sauce has cooked down and thickened and is brown in color. Pack hot sauce into hot jars, leaving ¼-inch headspace. Following the directions for water-bath canning in chapter 3, process half-pints and pints in a boiling water canner for 10 minutes at 0 to 1,000 feet; 15 minutes at 1,001 to 3,000 feet;

20 minutes at 3,001 to 6,000 feet; 25 minutes at 6,001 to 8,000 feet; 30 minutes above 8,000 feet. Makes about 7 to 8 pints.

This sauce is great on all kinds of meat. Try it as a glaze on meatloaf during the last 10 minutes.

Split Pea Soup

- 6 quarts dried split peas
- 6 quarts water
- 4½ cups carrots, diced
- 3 cups onion, chopped
- 3 cups cooked ham, diced
- ½ tsp. allspice
- Salt and pepper to taste

Preparing

In a large pot, combine split peas and water; bring to a boil. Reduce heat, cover, and simmer for 1 hour or until peas are soft. Mash peas, if desired, with a potato masher. Add remaining ingredients and simmer for 30 minutes. Adjust consistency of soup by adding boiling water or broth if needed.

Ladle hot soup into hot jars, leaving 1-inch headspace. Following the directions in chapter 4, "Pressure Canning—A Step-by-Step Guide," process quarts for 90 minutes and pints for 75 minutes at 10 psi, adjusting the psi as necessary for your altitude according to the altitude adjustment directions. Makes about 6 quarts.

Three-Meat Stew

- 1 quart beef,
- 1-inch cubes
- 1 quart lamb,
- 1-inch cubes
- 1½ quarts chicken,
- inch cubes
- 4 quarts potatoes, peeled and chunked
- 1 quart carrots, peeled and chunked, plus 1 carrot, peeled and cut in thirds (for cooking meat)
- 3 cups onions, chopped, plus 1 small onion, quartered (for cooking meat)

- 4 slices bacon, cut into thirds
- 1 green bell pepper, chunked
- 1 red bell pepper, chunked
- 3 cloves garlic, minced
- 1 T. black pepper
- 1 T. paprika
- 1 T. salt
- 1 pint tomato sauce
- ¾ cup tomato juice

Preparing

In a large pot, add meat, quartered onion, and carrot cut in thirds; cover with water and bring to a boil; reduce heat and simmer for about 1 hour, or until meat is cooked through and tender. Discard carrots and onion pieces.

Cook bacon and pour off grease. Add to the pot of meat. Add remaining ingredients to pot, cover, and simmer gently until mixture is hot. Ladle hot stew into hot jars, leaving 1-inch headspace. Following the pressure canning directions in chapter 4, process quarts for 90 minutes and pints for 75 minutes at 10 psi, adjusting the psi as necessary for your altitude according to the altitude adjustment directions. Makes about 9 to 10 quarts.

Quick And Easy Tomato Soup

- 3 cans (6 oz. each) tomato paste
- 3 quarts water
- 3 stalks celery, chunked into thirds
- 2 to 3 tsp. salt
- ¾ tsp. onion powder
- ½ tsp. garlic powder
- ¼–½ tsp. each, oregano, basil, thyme, rosemary, and celery seed
- 2 to 4 T. sugar (white or brown)
- 2 bay leaves (optional)

Preparing

In a large pot, mix all ingredients together and stir to mix. Bring to a boil and then simmer for 20 minutes. Take out the celery pieces and bay leaves. Taste and adjust seasonings if desired.

Ladle hot soup into hot pint jars, leaving 1-inch headspace. Following the pressure canning directions in chapter 4, process pints and quarts for 20 minutes at 10 psi, adjusting the psi as necessary for your altitude according to the altitude adjustment directions. Makes about 7 pints.

To serve: You can heat and serve as is, or you can add ½ cup cream or milk before heating. If you want thicker soup, melt 1 tablespoon butter in a saucepot; add 1 tablespoon flour and stir; while continuing to stir, pour in the pint of tomato soup and bring to a boil, all the while stirring so the flour doesn't lump. When the soup comes to a boil, the mixture will thicken. Remove from heat and immediately pour in ½ cup milk; stir and serve. Alternately, you can mix together ½ cup each dry milk powder and water and add that to your soup instead.

Fresh Tomato Soup

- 8 quarts fresh tomatoes (to make 5 to 6 quarts tomato puree)
- 6 onions, chopped

- 1 bunch celery, chopped

- 1 cup sugar

- 3 T. salt, or to taste

Preparing

Scald tomatoes by plunging them in boiling water for 30 to 45 seconds and then cold water to slip skins. (This step isn't necessary if you are using a Victorio strainer because it will remove the skin and seeds.) Remove tomato skins, chop in halves or quarters, and remove seeds and core. Put them in a large pot, add the chopped onion and celery, and cook on medium heat until tender, stirring regularly so they don't burn on the bottom of the pot. Run the tomato mixture through a food mill or strainer and return tomato pulp to the pot. Add sugar and salt and stir to mix and dissolve.

Ladle hot soup into hot jars, leaving 1-inch headspace. Following the pressure canning directions in chapter 4, process pints and quarts for 20 minutes at 10 psi, adjusting the psi as necessary for your altitude according to the altitude adjustment directions. Makes about 7 to 8 quarts.

To serve: You can heat and eat this as is, or you can add 1 tablespoon butter and ½ cup milk or cream per pint (2 tablespoons butter and 1 cup milk per quart) while heating.

Vegetarian Chili

- 2 cups dried kidney or pinto beans
- 5 lbs. tomatoes, skinned, seeded, and chopped
- 2 onions, chopped
- 6 cloves garlic, minced
- 1 green bell pepper, chopped
- 1 jalapeno pepper, chopped (wear gloves when handling hot pepper)
- 3 tsp. cumin
- 4 tsp. paprika
- 1 tsp. thyme
- 2 tsp. oregano
- 2 tsp. (or to taste) hot sauce

Preparing

In a pot, add beans and 2 quarts water. Bring to a boil and boil for 2 minutes. Remove from heat, cover, and let set for 1 hour. Rinse beans, return to pot with 2 quarts fresh water and simmer for 30 minutes.

In another large pot, add remainder of ingredients. Over medium heat and stirring frequently, bring to a boil; reduce heat and simmer for 20 minutes. Add drained beans and simmer another 10 minutes.

Ladle hot chili into hot jars, leaving ½-inch headspace. Following the pressure canning directions in chapter 4, process quarts for 90 minutes and pints for 75 minutes at 10 psi, adjusting the psi as necessary for your altitude according to the altitude adjustment directions. Makes about 5 quarts.

Chapter 13: Common Mistakes To Avoid When Canning

Canning is not difficult, and if you follow directions, it's rare that problems will occur. Some conditions in your canned food are not a problem (even though they might give you pause), and the food can be safely eaten; we'll talk about some of those later in this chapter. But if your jar of food shows any signs of spoilage—spurting liquid when you open the jar, indicating pressure; gas bubbles; soft, mushy, slimy, fermented, or moldy food; a fuzzy growth on top of the food; cloudy liquid; sediment in the liquid; leaking jars; broken or bulging seals; or off-color or -odor— don't taste the food. Instead, dispose of the food carefully:

- Wear gloves while handling the food and container.
- If the jar that contains suspected spoiled food still has a sealed cap, you may dispose of it in the trash or bury it in soil deep

enough that pets or wild animals can't smell it and dig up the contents.

- If the jar is leaking or the seal has broken, carefully place the jar with the food and the seal (take the seal off first) in a large pot. You can lay the jar on its side if you need to because you'll want to cover everything with water by an inch or two. As you are filling the pot, be careful not to splash water out of the pot. Cover the pot and bring to a boil. Boil the contents for 30 minutes, keeping the cover of the pot on at all times. Allow the contents to cool in the pot and then discard the food in the trash or bury in soil.

When you have disposed of the spoiled food, thoroughly wash and disinfect all surfaces nearby as well as all utensils and containers, still wearing your gloves. A good way to disinfect is to fill your sink with warm water and add ½ tsp. bleach for every gallon of water used. Set your utensils and pot into the sink and let them sit for five minutes. After they have sat in the solution for the allotted time, lay them out in a disinfected dish drainer or on a clean towel and allow to air dry. Another good way to disinfect surfaces (especially counters and stovetops) is to fill a spray bottle with water. Take the spray nozzle from the bottle and dip the stem in bleach, about three quarters of the way up the stem. Place the dipped stem in the spray bottle of water and swish around to get the bleach into the water. Repeat 2 more times. Then you can spray your surfaces until sopping wet (not damp) and allow them to air dry. If you decide to keep this spray bottle of disinfectant, please be sure to clearly mark the container so people know it's a bleach solution. Discard all gloves, sponges, and washcloths used.

There are also a number of conditions that can affect your canned food, but they are usually not considered dangerous. Keep in mind, however, that although certain color changes are usually benign, a color change accompanied by a foul or "off" odor indicates spoilage, and the food shouldn't be eaten. Instead, discard the contents as outlined above. Here is a list of some of the more common conditions you might encounter:

- Loss of liquid from the jar either during or after processing. If the jar has a good seal, the food is considered safe. Probable causes are rapid fluctuation of pressure in the canner, the food was packed too tightly, or air bubbles weren't removed before processing. If a water-bath canner was used, the water level may have dropped to below the top of the jars.

- Darkened food at top of jar. This usually occurs when liquid did not completely cover the food. If you have followed packing and processing instructions and no spoilage is present, the food is safe to eat.

- Fruit or tomatoes float in jar. If a sugar syrup was used, the fruit was lighter than the syrup. Can also occur with cold packing; hot-pack instead and pack fruit as closely as possible without crushing. Safe to eat.

- Black beets. Often caused by iron in the water used to process the food. If black beets are soft and the liquid murky, it's best to destroy the food as this could be an indication of spoilage.

- White or light beets. This occurs when the beets aren't fresh or a variety was used that isn't suitable for canning. The food is safe.

- Brown corn. This is generally the result of using super sweet corn varieties. The corn is safe to eat, but it's not attractive. Best to use known canning corn varieties.

- Green vegetables turning olive green or brown. This can result from the breakdown of chlorophyll in the food, overcooking, or canning too-mature vegetables. Safe to eat.

- Yellow crystals in asparagus. This is rutin, and doesn't affect the quality of the asparagus; the crystals usually dissolve when the food is heated, and is safe to eat.

- Yellow crystals on canned green vegetables. This is formed by naturally occurring glucoside in the vegetables. Safe to eat.

- White crystals on canned spinach. This is a calcium oxalate precipitate and the food is safe to eat.

- White sediment on bottom of jars. This usually indicates that the starch has settled out of the food or that hard water was used to process. The food is safe to eat. However, it could indicate bacterial spoilage if the entire liquid contents are cloudy and the food is soft. In this situation, destroy the food.

- Blue, pink, purple, or red color in canned apples, pears, peaches, and quinces. This is a natural chemical change from the heat and the food is safe to eat. These color changes vary depending on the variety of fruit used.

- Crystals in grape products. This is tartaric acid (think cream of tartar) and is perfectly safe, but may be unpalatable. If grape juice, you can strain the juice to remove the crystals.

- Jelly is moldy. Indicates improper seal. Do not use.

- Bubbles in jelly. If the bubbles are moving, jelly is spoiling; do not use. If the bubbles remain in place, this often occurs from ladling the jelly into the jars from too high up; hold the ladle close to the jar opening while slowly pouring.

- Corroded lids, dark color on inside surface of lid. This happens most often with high-acid foods. Usually not a problem, unless the seal has been compromised due to extensive corrosion.

- Black, brown, or gray colors in food. Chemical reaction with minerals present in water or utensils. Try using soft water, and avoid using copper, iron, or chipped enamel utensils.

- Pinholes in fish. This is often due to fish worms, but can also occur when the fish has been held for too long before processing. If the jars are sealed and you know the fish was processed properly, it's safe to eat, but the quality will be reduced. Better to buy your fish from a reputable dealer and to process it as soon as possible.

- Blackening in tuna, chicken, or turkey. Avoid iodized salt when canning and don't use iron containers or pots when preparing meats, poultry, or fish for canning. The food is safe to eat, but unattractive.

- Meat products have little broth. Probable causes are pressure fluctuations while canning, causing liquid to siphon out of the jar, or not enough liquid added to the food when the jars were packed. The food is safe to eat, but the meat may be dry.

Remember: When in doubt, throw it out.

These lists might cause a check in your enthusiasm, but the reality is that you can put up hundreds of jars of food and never experience most of what's listed. The Centers for Disease Control and Prevention (CDC) website reports: From 1999 to 2008, 116 outbreaks of food-borne botulism were reported. Of the 48 outbreaks caused by home-prepared foods from the contiguous United States, 38% (18) were from home-canned vegetables. Three outbreaks of Type A botulism occurred in Ohio and Washington in September 2008, January 2009, and June 2009. Home-canned vegetables (green beans, green bean and carrot blend, and asparagus) served at family meals were confirmed as the source of each outbreak. In each instance, home canners did not follow canning instructions, did not use pressure cookers, ignored signs of food spoilage, and were unaware of the risk of botulism from consuming improperly preserved vegetables.

One hundred sixteen reported cases during a ten-year period is low, in my opinion—but of course, low isn't good enough if it's your family who suffers. But notice that in each of the three outbreaks of Type A botulism reported, the problem seems to have been that the food wasn't properly processed. That's a preventable statistic. By carefully following directions and using the proper equipment, canning really is a safe way to preserve food. And there has been so much research done over the course of many years on the subject of safely preserving our food that we can be confident of our success in the canning kitchen.

Wow! If you're looking to get my other books, click the link below;

Emily Fisher's Books

Don't forget to leave your honest review, thanks!

Chapter 14: A Word Of Encouragement

I'm sitting here at my computer on a dreary early winter day, and while it may be miserable outside, in the house here I'm warm and cozy. I've got a canner load of black beans soaking, which I plan to process later this afternoon, and I just pulled out a jar of tomato soup from the pantry, which will pair nicely with my grilled cheese sandwich for lunch.

The main push of preserving is over for the year, and my shelves are brimming. I'll continue to put up food from time to time during the winter, but for now, I'm satisfied. The joy I get from knowing that my pantry is full and the satisfaction I have when I contemplate that those packed shelves are mostly due to my hard work over the course of the summer just can't be equaled.

Thinking ahead, I realize christmas is just around the corner. I'll order the largest turkey my budget allows, and all of my sons, daughters and family will show up, hungry and ready to dig into the favorite family recipes. We'll eat and visit, and at the end of the day, we'll head home to bed. But my day won't be quite over. Because as sure as christmas comes every year, so does my urge to boil the turkey bones until they yield their rich and tasty broth—and I'll get out my trusty pressure canner and put up a load or two of turkey meat and broth to see me through the winter months.

Canning is really good!

If you'd like to know me more, I am presently not a social media fan; I was recently introduced to amazon by a friend of mine. I am an author of 5 books on amazon, if you want to get in touch with me, follow my amazon author page, thanks! I'll see you again in my next book, Bye!

About The Author

Emily Fisher is proprietor at Magnolia Bakery and a certified master food preserver. She teaches people how to prepare and preserve healthy foods, live simply with integrity, and get the most from what they have.

She also brings the handmade essence of Magnolia Bakery to customers through the creation and development of new recipes and the perfection of old favorites.

Note